life, no matter where He takes you. You will read it, as I have, and be reminded of His great grace."

Madelyn Edens,
missionary emeritus to the Middle East,
International Mission Board,
Southern Baptist Convention

"Shelby's book is one that I do not recommend that you begin reading at nine in the evening—unless you want to be up all night. Yes, trite as the phrase may sound, *Behind the Veils of Yemen* is one of those can't-put-down books.

"Shelby prayed—not just in morning devotions but throughout her day—and learned to give thanks in all things. She writes with an honesty about her struggles, failures and victories that gives glory to God for what she and her husband saw happen in Yemen. Her book is one I highly recommend—if you want a challenge to pray more, give more and perhaps even go to someplace where people have yet to hear the Good News that Jesus saves!"

Aretta Loving,
former translator and current writer and speaker,
Wycliffe Bible Translators, Papua New Guinea;
author, Slices of Life: Stories and Devotions from a Bible Translator *and* Together We Can! A Mosaic of Stories
and Devotions Displaying the Impact of God's Word

"Audra Shelby's sharing is powerful and heartfelt, impacting and educating audiences for whom Islam—especially from a woman's unique point of view—would otherwise remain a mystery. I was deeply moved not only by her personal experience but also in my own spiritual walk."

Lori Koch,
ministry leader and former missionary

"This is a compelling tale, skillfully told, of a young family embarking upon an extraordinary adventure with God and both the struggles and victories that infuse their lives of faith. With rare sensitivity, Shelby introduces readers to the lovely country and people of Yemen, particularly the women who live and love unveiled beyond the walls. As she brings to life this fascinating culture with riveting detail and charming poignancy, she creates a hunger to experience the world of the Middle East, God's activity in it and how He leads those who choose to walk in His ways."

Karen O'Dell Bullock, Ph.D.;
professor of Christian heritage and
director of Ph.D. program,
B. H. Carroll Theological Institute

"The story enclosed within the pages of this book invites a reader to take a fascinating faith journey with a young missionary family in Yemen as recounted through the pen of Audra Shelby. You will journey along with Audra and discover that your senses come alive through sights, smells and sounds as well as joys and sorrows that have lain behind both real and figurative veils for centuries. Let a reader take good care! You will be drawn quickly into her story as though you were living it with her and find your heart beating with new gospel vibrancy as her pioneering path invites you to follow closely in her steps."

Larry C. Ashlock, D.Min., Ph.D.;
professor of pastoral leadership and ethics
and director of D.Min program,
B. H. Carroll Theological Institute

"Most of us here in America have a fear of the Muslim people and what we believe they represent. This is an insightful book written from a Christian perspective on the Muslim world with a compassionate heart. It removed some of that fear and enabled me to have a genuine concern for Muslims and also gave me a greater understanding of God's love and grace toward me. Everyone should read it!"

Harold Velasquez, vice president,
US Hispanic Ministries,
Mike Silva International

"This book genuinely reflects the ups and downs in the life of any missionary who serves in a restricted country that is drastically different culturally, religiously, politically and economically from his or her own country. The trials and frustrations, as well as the excitement of experiencing the joy of God's provision, care and love, are well expressed. In a beautiful and candid style, Audra captures the interest of the reader and takes him or her on the journey into the Lord's ministry."

Samuel Shahid, Ph.D.,
senior professor of Islamic studies,
Southwestern Baptist Theological Seminary

"Americans have a stereotypical concept of Islamic culture that reflects their own ethnocentric cultural bondage. Audra Shelby, with her husband and three small children, not only ventured to live within a Muslim society; they sought to understand and penetrate the hearts of those to whom they hoped to introduce God's love. Insights into the strong beliefs of others forced them to see their own convictions in a new perspective. The personal trials and challenges they encountered gave them a glimpse into God's faithfulness, power and grace beyond what they had previously known. *Behind the Veils of Yemen* will captivate the reader with intrigue and a new dimension of faith and commitment."

Jerry Rankin, president emeritus,
International Mission Board,
Southern Baptist Convention

"Audra is one of several women who have been instrumental in addressing women and mothers in the Islamic world. She provided leadership in developing a strategy for an unreached Islamic people group with little or no access to the Gospel before her family began their ministry among them. She writes with this unique knowledge and experience as her context. I am blessed to call her friend and co-worker."

Michael H. Edens,
professor of theology and Islamic studies
and associate dean of graduate studies,
New Orleans Baptist Theological Seminary;
associate director, Institute of Christian Apologetics

"This book gives you a glimpse behind the scenes with real, live missionaries. Audra shares her deepest fears and thoughts as she interacts with the Muslim culture and religion. If you want to know how God calls and uses missionaries in very difficult situations to share the Good News, this book is a must-read."

Avery Willis, executive director,
International Orality Network;
former vice president, Overseas Operations,
International Mission Board,
Southern Baptist Convention

"Audra has great concern for the Islamic women she lived among for many years. Those concerns have translated into action. She often speaks to groups about her experiences in the Middle East and is always upbeat and positive in the images she conveys to her audiences. Her deep understanding of her Christian beliefs and the knowledge she has gained about the role of women in the Islamic faith allow her to speak with love and compassion. I am honored to have a woman with her breadth and depth of experiences as my friend."

C. Ray Warrior,
former IT executive

"Intriguing story! Knowing that God uses the weak to intimidate the strong, this mission work with Middle Eastern women may be an essential step in God's final plans for redemption of the world."

Dr. Deborah Gunderman, D.Min.;
founder, Walking in the Way, Inc.

"For a modern American woman, following Christ as she raises her family is always an adventure. Sometimes it's smooth; often not. So what happens when that adventure with God takes a woman to a far and difficult land and through heartbreaking family experiences? You will find that this book is not about the strength of a woman's heart or even of her faith. This is a story, again, of God's goodness in all of

Behind the Veils of Yemen

How an American Woman Risked Her Life, Family and Faith to Bring Jesus to Muslim Women

Audra Grace Shelby

Chosen

a division of Baker Publishing Group
Grand Rapids, Michigan

Published by Chosen Books
11400 Hampshire Avenue South
Bloomington, MN 55438
www.chosenbooks.com

Chosen Books is a division of
Baker Publishing Group, Grand Rapids, Michigan

Printed in the United States of America

Library of Congress Cataloging-in-Publication Data
Shelby, Audra Grace.
    Behind the veils of Yemen : how an American woman risked her life,
  family, and faith to bring Jesus to Muslim women / Audra Grace Shelby.
       p.   cm.
    ISBN 978-0-8007-9518-4
    1. Shelby, Audra Grace. 2. Missions to Muslims—Yemen (Republic).
  3. Church Work with women—Yemen (Republic). 4. Muslim women—
  Religious life—Yemen (Republic). 5. Missionaries—Yemen (Republic)—
  Biography. 6. Missionaries—United States—Biography. I. Title.
  BV3210.Y4S54 2011
  266′.6092—dc23   2011025239

Cover design by Dan Pitts

11 12 13 14 15 16 17   7 6 5 4 3 2 1

In keeping with biblical principles of creation stewardship, Baker Publishing Group advocates the responsible use of our natural resources. As a member of the Green Press Initiative, our company uses recycled paper when possible. The text paper of this book is composed in part of post-consumer waste.

To my Lord, the God of all creation,
who gives the mouth the ability to speak
and knows all thoughts before they are words.
You chose me, and I remain overwhelmed.
This book is for You,
that others may know You as I have known You.
To my husband,
who believes in me when I do not,
who is the keel God placed to upright my life,
and who is my love and my greatest birthday present ever.
To my four children,
who have brought me joy from the moment I held them.
This is their legacy.
May they never forget.

Jeremiah 17:5–8

Acknowledgments

As a child blossoms within a community, so this book has blossomed through the encouragement and support of many. I remain humbly grateful for contributions of time, encouragement, prayer and guidance. Each contribution has helped to grow *Behind the Veils of Yemen* and blessed me in the process. Hoping that each contributor will see beyond the limit of mere words, I thank each with endless gratitude.

I thank my family, for praying me through every step. I thank them for patiently understanding my need to write, for providing me time to write and for believing in what I was writing. I thank them for their editorial eyes and comments, their excitement and their limitless encouragement. I thank them most for their steadfast faith in our Lord.

I thank friends who affirmed me in doubtful moments. When I presented the first chapters, they asked for more and then urged and prayed me onward. When opportunities seemed daunting, they prayed with me for open doors.

I also thank friends who provided technical expertise as they helped develop my electronic world and introduced me to websites and social networks.

I thank those who took time from busy schedules to read and recommend my book. Their recommendations were blessings showered on a thirsty author, and I am grateful and honored by each one. These special people have been instrumental in my life—equipping me, inspiring me, walking with me, wanting others to hear my story. I pray that they will be blessed by the blessing they have bestowed.

I give special recognition to Dr. Avery Willis, who took time during the final two weeks of his life to read, encourage and endorse the work of this first-time author. I will never forget his kindness.

I also thank the staff at Chosen Books and Baker Publishing who have blessed and carried me through each step of the publishing process. They opened the door and patiently guided me through it; they cared about my preferences in every phase; they guarded and guided me with their editorial skills; and they have been a joy to work with always.

Above all, I thank my Lord and praise Him for guiding this book to fruition. Without Him, there would simply be no story to tell.

1

Our three children stared at the white-robed figures walking down the narrow aisle to join our flight from Amsterdam to Yemen. My husband, Kevin, and I tried to study them more discreetly. We pretended not to watch as they settled into their assigned seats.

"Say thank-you," I directed as Madison took an activity pack from the flight attendant.

Madison thanked her and examined a coloring book while Jack played with a folding toothbrush. I thanked another flight attendant for a magazine I did not read. My eyes were on the white-robed group who were buckling their seatbelts for takeoff.

Most in the group were men, talking and laughing together. Some were chanting quietly over strands of prayer beads they clicked between their fingers. A few were women who had been escorted by their husbands to vacant window seats. Their husbands sat next to them in protective aisle seats, blocking out the seats between them. The men were draped in white. Some wore velvety robes fastened at their shoulders by hidden clasps, while others wore what appeared to be bedsheets that threatened to slip from knots at their waists. These were frequently adjusted, exposing bare chests underneath.

The few women were veiled in black from head to toe. Black gloves covered their hands, and black opaque socks hid their ankles. The briefest wedge of brown eyes and olive skin peeked from their veils.

I made eye contact with a woman one row back and smiled. "Good afternoon," I murmured.

I could not tell if she smiled back or frowned under her veil. She did not answer, but her eyes held mine steadily until my daughter tugged at my sleeve, calling me back to the story I had promised to read.

The men were Muslim pilgrims bound for the most sacred of Islamic shrines to perform the most sacred of its rites: circling the Kaaba and kissing the stone they believed to be at the center of the world. I watched the men intent in their Arabic conversation.

"How long do you think the spiritual high from the *hajj* will satisfy you? Will it be enough?" I wanted to ask. I wondered if they were seeking God or simply pursuing self-fulfillment.

I braced my back against the seat as the plane raised its nose into the sky. We were in our final flight to the Middle East, only a few hours from descent into its heart.

"Is our next stop Yemen, Mommy?" Madison looked up from her dot-to-dot page.

"No, baby. We stop in Jeddah first, in Saudi Arabia. Then we go on to Yemen."

I thought back to the predawn flight we had boarded in Texas the day before. I had not realized how hard it would be to tell our families good-bye. Our pain in leaving had doubled when we saw their pain in letting us go.

My brother's voice had broken when our flight had been called. "I will pray for you every day of the next four years."

He had choked me in a gripping hug. "Please come back to us safely." I had not been able to answer with the cheerful words I had used among church friends. I knew that my mother's death on the mission field 34 years earlier was in my brother's tears.

"God will be with us, Alan," I had whispered. "He will be enough for what lies ahead." Kevin and I had nudged the children away from their grandparents' tearful grips and had moved them down the Jetway.

In Dallas we had transitioned to our first international flight. I had wanted to seize that minute, freeze the second that we were jetted away from all that was left of our comfortable lives. Twilight had darkened the American landscape receding in the distance. It had closed the day behind us as if closing a book.

The Dutch flight attendant held out her tray, bringing me back to the present. "Would you like orange juice or water?" she whispered in the darkened cabin.

I thanked her for the juice, straightening my cramped legs in my economy-class seat. After thirty hours of travel, my body ached with fatigue.

"How much longer is it to Jeddah?" I whispered to her.

"Less than two hours now. But you are going to Yemen, yes?" She looked passed me at Madison and Jack, who were both asleep.

I nodded and began to explain. "We are moving there."

The excitement in my eyes faded when I saw the frown in hers. I sipped my juice as she moved away down the aisle.

I cuddled two-year-old Jack, who had fallen asleep half on me and half on his seat beside me. His cottony hair wisped across his toddler head. Seven-year-old Madison slept against my other side, her sandy hair waving softly around her china doll face. I tucked the navy blanket around her small shoulders.

I looked over at Kevin in the adjoining row. His head was nodding against his headrest. Our five-year-old son, Jaden, clutched his yellow teddy bear, Shoobie, and slept soundly against Kevin's arm, blond hair curling like a cap around his chubby face. Kevin's Middle East travel guides had slipped to the floor, and the book he had been reading to Jaden was about to join them.

I leaned back against my own headrest and closed my eyes. Words from a well-meaning friend echoed into my ear. "How can you take those babies to live in a place like that?"

I tucked the blankets closer around Madison and Jack and swatted at the invading thoughts, but they returned like buzzing flies. I bent to kiss Madison's cheek.

"What will the next four years hold for you?" I whispered.

I stroked her hair, still soft and fine like a baby's. How would she feel in an Arab world ruled by men who placed little value on females? I looked discreetly back at the veiled woman I had greeted. Her hair covering had loosened around her head. She was staring out of her small window into the endless black night. Her husband snored beside her.

I swallowed the last of my orange juice wondering how my hair would look after hours under a binding scarf. I brushed at a tea stain on my dress. A summer night two years earlier flashed through my mind.

"I think God might be calling me to serve overseas." Kevin's words had resonated with the cicadas we had been listening to on the back patio.

"Are you sure?" I had sputtered, spilling my entire cup of hot tea on my pants.

Kevin had been sure, but I had not. I had wrestled with insecurity, wondering why the Lord would want to use *me*. Hardly missionary material, I was impulsive and opinionated and had left a wake of mistakes in my turbulent teens and twenties. It had been difficult to grasp that God wanted to use someone like me. Why He did was beyond me. But I had learned that was the point. It was beyond me. He had chosen me not because of who I was, but because of who He is.

I adjusted my loose denim dress to keep from flashing my calves to the white-robed men in the row next to me. I was determined to present myself as modest as their women, dressing as they defined modesty. I glanced back at the veiled woman's coverings and sighed. It would not be easy. I liked clothes that flattered what I worked hard to keep in shape.

I gritted my teeth. *I'll do it, Lord. I won't profane Your name by flaunting my freedoms, even if it's just showing my brown hair and my freckled arms.*

Madison stirred and I gently shifted her, worried about her legs in their cramped, curled position. Again my thoughts accused me. *How could I take my children from their home and jet them to a third-world country half a globe away?*

I bit my lip, remembering my apprehension when we knew God was calling us to Yemen. I had envisioned an easier place, such as a village near a beach in the Caribbean. But God was leading us to a place plagued with poverty and sickness and strict adherence to Islamic law, a place where evangelism was forbidden. I had dug in my heels.

"Kevin, I'm not sure we should raise our children in a place like Yemen. Look how many children die before they are six! It could be dangerous for them as well as us."

"Lord," I had argued. "You could not want to take our children away from all the U.S. can provide!"

I had refused to accept that not only did God love my children more than I did, He also had created them for His purposes, not for mine. I had wrestled until I could make no other choice but to obey or disobey God's call to Yemen. And then I had submitted, reluctantly. I had unclenched my fists and my teeth and acknowledged that God was not only calling my husband to serve, He was also calling me.

"Okay, Lord," I had muttered. "I will go wherever You lead. Even to Yemen, the uttermost part of the earth."

After I had crossed that line of obedience, God answered my apprehensions. They became like bread crumbs I had tried to hold on to, until one day at a hospital in Virginia God let me glimpse the banquet table He wanted to give me instead.

I felt around my lap for my missing tissue as tears threatened to well again in my tired eyes. I wiped what was left of my two-day-old mascara and tucked the tissue into my bulging seat pocket.

"Thank You, Father, for those days in Virginia," I prayed. "I could not have done this without them."

I clutched Madison and Jack closer to me. I closed my eyes and in my mind went back to that hospital, where Kevin's dying body lay tossing in his ICU bed, his IV lines inadequate to save him.

"I need to remember," I whispered. "When I get anxious, Lord, help me remember."

We had flown into Richmond at the onset of a crisp fall night full of mist from a recent rainfall. The International Mission Board had invited us to the Candidate's Conference, and we had left the children with special friends from church. I had been hesitant to leave Jack, who was still nursing, but he was fifteen months old and the conference would last only four days. We were excited as we anticipated completing the application process and being selected for appointment.

"We will be called oaks of righteousness, a planting of the Lord to display His splendor," I had told Kevin when we received the letter inviting us to our conference.

Kevin had raised his eyebrows.

"My verse for today," I explained. "Isaiah 61:3."

My excitement grew as we navigated the Richmond roads that were wet and black in the headlights of the van shuttling us from the airport. Spiky arms of stripped-down trees pointed the entrance to the hotel. We drove in and unloaded, crunching dead leaves underfoot as we rolled our luggage toward the lobby. The autumn night felt chilly, but I do not remember whether I shivered more from the cold or from my anticipation of the events that lay ahead.

We met other missionary candidates at the check-in counter. We all seemed to be talking more than we would in different circumstances and laughing at things that at another place and time would not have been funny. Those standing next to us began to share information about the places they would serve and the positions they would fill. We did the same, swapping photos of our children as we waited for room keys.

Inside our room, Kevin and I tore into the information packet we had received at check-in.

"What is on the schedule for tomorrow?" I scoured the packet over Kevin's shoulder.

The conference schedule was full, with little time between appointments and seminars. The day we faced the next morning would be no exception. We were scheduled for psychiatric interviews at eight, followed by complete physical exams and meetings that extended into the evening.

Kevin studied the Richmond map. "Looks like Old Marle Road is the quickest way to the psychiatrist's office."

I nodded as I pressed my khaki trousers with a steam iron. I left navigation responsibilities to Kevin. I could get lost in my own neighborhood. I finished ironing, and we readied ourselves for bed, turning off the light by eleven. We were determined to be rested, with our mental capacities at their best.

Two hours later I awoke to hear Kevin vomiting in the bathroom. "The potato soup," I groaned. Kevin had eaten it at an airport buffet. The soup had been only lukewarm, but selections had been slim and we had been hungry, so Kevin had eaten it anyway.

My second thought was aggravation. "How are we going to have good exams with no sleep?" I grudgingly shuffled to the bathroom to offer Kevin a wet washcloth and cold water.

Again and again through the night Kevin dashed for the bathroom, his vomiting accompanied by diarrhea. With increasing irritation, I offered him wet washcloths and sips of cool water. Dawn seemed a long time coming, but it finally arrived, brimming with sunshine.

I blinked at the light and blinked at Kevin, groaning as I threw back the covers. Both of us looked as if we had been up most of the night. Kevin had begun running a fever, but his vomiting and diarrhea had subsided, so I breathed prayers of relief as I showered and dressed.

I struggled to get contact lenses into my stinging blue eyes and shook Kevin gently to wake him again. "Honey, do you think you'll be able to make the meeting this morning?" I asked.

"Yeah, yeah," he muttered, trying to sit himself up in the bed. "I'll be okay. I'm just tired from all that time in the bathroom."

I laid out the clothes he wanted to wear. Assured that he could shower and dress himself, I left to grab breakfast in the hotel coffee shop. Kevin was all too glad to stay behind and avoid restaurant smells. He was weak and moving slowly, but he was moving.

Twenty minutes later I opened the door to find that not only was Kevin not dressed, he was stretched out on the bed sleeping. I was stunned. Kevin was a man who defined punctuality as fifteen minutes early. He was never late; he left that function to me.

"Kevin, we have to leave in five minutes and you're not even dressed!" I yelled, grabbing his shirt and trousers. I hesitated. "Are you okay, honey? Are you feeling sick again? Do we need to call someone and postpone our appointments?"

Kevin shook his head and mumbled an apology as he slowly pulled himself from the bed. "I'm okay. I didn't think I would fall back asleep," he admitted sheepishly.

I quickly helped him dress, glancing at the bedside clock. I could feel the heat from his feverish body as I buttoned his shirt. I stashed our schedule packet into my purse and helped Kevin put on his tie and sports jacket. We shuffled slowly down the corridor, Kevin's six-foot body leaning heavily on my five-foot-three frame.

We inched our way through dead leaves in the parking lot and found the rental car that Kevin was supposed to drive. I settled him into the passenger seat and sighed as I got behind the steering wheel.

I waved the map at Kevin. "Can you help me find the road where we are supposed to turn?" I asked in a growing panic. "I don't mind driving, but you know how I am with directions. Do I go straight on this street and then turn left, or do I turn first and go straight at the light?" I screeched out of the hotel parking lot in what I hoped was the right direction.

Kevin took the map slowly from my waving hand and tried to focus on it. He steadied his head against the head-rest and turned the map crosswise, but he could not seem to read it. He mumbled something I could not understand. I was growing more frustrated.

"Honey, I need to know where to turn!" I pleaded.

"I'm sorry, sweetheart." He spoke slowly and with effort, then handed the map back to me. "I can't make it out. My head is all foggy."

He leaned back against the seat and closed his eyes. "I'm sorry you're having to handle all of this." His words were drawn out and labored. "I'm no help, am I?"

In spite of my inclination to agree, I patted his arm. "That's okay, honey. You just rest and take it easy. I'll get us there."

I'll get us there, I repeated to myself. *I can do this.* I took a deep breath, willing myself to focus.

Kevin dozed in and out as I made one wrong turn after another. I finally delivered us to the psychiatrist's home, twenty minutes late for our appointment.

As we got out of the car, I whispered to Kevin, "I hope being late isn't rooted in some deep psychiatric problem." He smiled weakly in response.

Entering the psychiatrist's home office, I tried to appear calmer and more collected than I was. I apologized sheepishly for getting lost.

The psychiatrist looked closely at Kevin. "It's a good thing your next exam is at the hospital clinic," he said.

Kevin was coherent throughout the interview, and we completed it smoothly together, answering a barrage of questions about our childhood and adolescence. We apparently passed the evaluation in spite of ourselves.

Outside we were joined by another candidate. I was only too glad to relinquish the car keys. I climbed into the backseat as Kevin slept in the front. We passed oak trees denuded of once abundant leaves. They stood resolute between the quiet old brownstones of Richmond and lifted pitiful limbs to the sky, as if they knew their nakedness was necessary before thick foliage could grow.

We arrived at the hospital clinic on time for our appointments. I sighed with relief as I seated Kevin and myself in the reception area and began filling out registration forms. I completed mine and worked on Kevin's while he slept, slumped in the chair beside me. I was trying to remember his family information when Kevin uttered a guttural moan, interrupting my concentration. I glanced from my clipboard to Kevin. He was leaning forward, his pupils like tiny black dots in his opened green eyes.

I sent the clipboards flying as I lunged for the registration desk. "Something's wrong with my husband!" I shouted at the receptionist.

The startled clerk jumped in irritated surprise. But when she saw Kevin slumped in his seat with his eyes open and unseeing, she hit the intercom immediately.

"Code Blue, Admissions. Code Blue, Admissions."

Everything whirred together in a blur of white and green as hospital staff appeared instantly beside us. A doctor in scrubs stretched Kevin out on the floor, loosening his belt, unbuttoning his shirt, and listening to his heart all at the same time. A nurse in white took his blood pressure while firing a volley of questions at me. I stared in disbelief, stumbling through a description of the previous night and explaining that we were there to see Dr. Valdadoss in the clinic.

Kevin awoke and attempted to sit up, protesting weakly at the attention. "I'm okay. I'm okay," he said, trying to brush the nurse aside. His sixty-over-thirty blood pressure reading disagreed.

"Lie down, sir." The emergency room doctor motioned for an orderly with a gurney. They helped Kevin onto it and wheeled him away from the reception area with me following closely behind. I tried to ask questions, but the words would not come. My legs were moving in pace with the hospital staff, but I could not feel them.

As the doors pushed open to the clinic, the nursing staff gasped in surprise. "Oh, my!" exclaimed Libby, Dr. Valdadoss's nurse.

"What happened?" Dr. Valdadoss hurried to us in answer to his page.

I gave a hasty explanation of the night before. Dr. Valdadoss wheeled Kevin into a room and examined him as he nodded at my answers to his questions.

"Kevin is dehydrated, probably from a touch of food poisoning." Dr. Valdadoss hung his stethoscope back around his neck. "No more cold potato soup." He smiled at Kevin.

Libby walked in with an IV bag. Dr. Valdadoss turned to me. "We need to admit him to the hospital for 24 hours and get him rehydrated," he said. "He is running a high fever and we need to bring that down and get him stabilized. Then he'll be as good as new."

Seeing the shock on my face, Dr. Valdadoss patted my arm. "Tomorrow he'll be a different man," he said. "He'll be fine."

Libby inserted an IV into Kevin's arm and helped the attendant prepare to wheel him from the clinic to the hospital wing. I moved to follow them.

"Mrs. Shelby, you need to stay here until we get him settled into a room," Libby stopped me. "Since you are here, you might as well finish your physical and get your part done." She held out my medical forms.

I clutched the end of the gurney with one hand and slowly reached for the forms with the other. I tightened my grip, wanting to stay with my husband, but feeling compelled to comply. I reluctantly stepped back as they wheeled my husband away.

"Take care of him, Lord," I whispered.

When I was done, blue arrows painted on the shiny floor of the corridor directed me from the clinic to the hospital. I paused at a small pharmacy in between them. I glanced at my watch and went in to purchase a breast pump, something I had forgotten at home. It had been more than 24 hours since I had nursed Jack, and I was beginning to feel our separation.

The redheaded cashier wore a lab coat splashed with orange and fuchsia flowers. She handed me my change as she put the pump in a paper sack. My absentminded answers to her pleasant questions sparked apparently hungry conversation.

"You're not from around here, are you, honey?" she asked, handing me my sack. "I can tell by your accent. Have you been out on the town yet? Don't you leave Richmond without having a good time, you hear?"

The tears exploded out of me before I could stop them. I could not answer the astonished woman as her mouth dropped open and her eyes blinked wide and repeatedly. She grabbed a tissue box behind the counter and handed me a handful.

"Are you all right, honey? Can I get you a drink of water or something? Do you need a chair to sit down?"

I shook my head no. I choked out my thanks for the tissues and mumbled a few words about Kevin. Blaming my fatigue, I apologized and backed out of the pharmacy. I gulped deep breaths, struggling to get my tears under control. I leaned against the corridor wall. I willed myself to breathe, squeezing my eyes shut to stop the tears. I gripped my hands together until my trembling subsided. I dabbed my face with tissues and smoothed a hand over my clothes and hair. *The worst is over,* I told myself. *Kevin is where he needs to be. Tomorrow things will be better.* I took another deep breath. *I am strong enough to do this, right, Lord?* I threw a glance upward. I fumbled around in my purse for lipstick and steadied my hand to smear it in place. I slowly resumed my pace down the hall.

2

Kevin smiled weakly as I walked into his private room. Relief washed over his face like a wave smoothing trampled sand. I kissed his hot forehead and squeezed his hand. His body felt hotter.

"Some day this was," he said with effort.

"Yeah, it's preparing us for all the stomach troubles we're going to have overseas." I tried to grin, glancing at his overhead monitor. His temperature was hovering at 105 and his blood pressure was staying around 60 over 40.

The door opened, and a nurse came in with a large, gel-filled rectangle. "Mrs. Shelby? I'm Sarah, your husband's afternoon nurse. I'm going to put him on a cooling blanket to bring his fever down. Can you help me get it under him?"

I helped Kevin roll sideways, and together Sarah and I slid the pad underneath him. I tried to keep my eyes off Sarah's worried brown ones as she checked the readings on his monitor. She was in her late thirties, with bobbed brown hair and a blue uniform. She wrote notes on her chart then left the room.

Kevin continued to drift in and out of sleep. His eyes fluttered open to find me and closed when they had. I sat on his bed, letting him squeeze the hand he would not release.

The afternoon poured sun through the window and I was grateful for it, eager for a glimpse of something natural and familiar. I left Kevin's bedside to let the sunlight wash over me through the tinted glass. I could not see the sun; the wall from the next wing was blocking it. But I knew it was there. I could feel its warmth and see the light streaming from it.

Sarah began to return every fifteen minutes. Kevin's temperature was not going down. Sarah's worried eyes were joined by tightening lips and an occasional shaking head. Kevin's body seemed to be swelling. His face looked puffy and bloated. He had received several liters of IV fluid, but I noticed that his catheter bag was empty. He was not passing the fluids he received.

I began to leave my chair more frequently to pace around the room. My pace was beginning to match Sarah's as she came in and out to check Kevin's monitor. I was growing impatient. I was ready for Kevin to respond to the IV fluids and bounce quickly back like the doctor had said he would, but it was not happening. Kevin was not getting better. He was getting worse, and Sarah knew it.

The day began to end. As the afternoon sun finished pouring its shine through the window, a shadow, growing from the outside wall, slowly mopped the light away. It made the room appear dark and full of gloom, so I closed the curtains and switched on an extra light. I tried to squelch my growing uneasiness with thoughts about our children at home. I wondered what they were doing and how Jack was adjusting without me. I told myself my fears were in my head and I was only imagining Kevin getting worse. I gritted my teeth and whispered that Kevin would get better if I believed hard enough. So I willed him to heal, not recognizing whose will my faith was pursuing. Kevin began to sleep for longer periods. Sarah became visibly more agitated. She no longer attempted to hide the frustration in her voice. She began to murmur things under her breath that I could not hear. I tried to encourage her, to tell her Kevin was improving, but I knew he was not.

Finally Sarah turned from the monitor and faced me "I'm sorry, Mrs. Shelby, but I called Dr. Valdadoss. Your husband needs to be in the ICU. I can't give him the care he needs, and I don't want to take responsibility for him. Dr. Valdadoss is transferring him to the ICU as soon as they prepare a bed." She walked brusquely from the room without looking back at Kevin or me.

My head began to spin as Dr. Valdadoss appeared and a new group of nurses, equipment and talk murmured around Kevin. A nurse named Kalyn asked me to leave while they prepared my husband for the transfer. She told me they would call me after Kevin was settled into the ICU.

I felt numb and moved in a daze. Feeling powerless, I voiced no opposition. I was out of his room without realizing I had walked out. Through the door I heard Kalyn tell Dr. Valdadoss that she could not insert another IV. Kevin's veins had collapsed.

As I groped my way to the ICU waiting room, I tried to grasp what was happening. Kevin was supposed to have food poisoning. He was simply supposed to recover. "It can't be more than that!" I gritted my teeth and slumped down into an armchair, leaning against its burly cushions. The beige walls of the room surrounded me like a net waiting for prey, the hazy watercolors hanging on each side like bait attracting helpless people who could do nothing but bide their time. I kicked the carpet.

"I won't be caught by circumstances, and I won't sit helpless in any waiting room!" I jumped from my chair and paced the nearest hallway.

My shoes slapped each shiny tile as I marched down hall after hall. Thoughts in my head began to spin like a brightly painted top—faster and faster like a blur of confused colors that would not stop or slow to allow clarity. I tried to pray but could not; the words were trapped in the whirl of spinning thoughts. I knew God was there, but I could not focus enough to find Him. All my years of prayer and meditation escaped me. Even the strength I thought I had within myself was stripped away. My will was not enough. I could not make myself think, and I could not grasp what to do. I whirled helplessly in circumstances I could not control.

I craved a place where I could be alone to sort my whirling thoughts. I felt desperate for a closet, a private place where I could force my spinning thoughts into focus, but I could not find it. Nurses and doctors scurried through endlessly long halls. Waiting rooms held listless people and chattering televisions. Corners were crowded with newspaper stands and soda machines. I could not find an unlocked closet. I could not find a solitary place to find what I so desperately lacked.

My pace quickened to the point that I was almost running. I was nearly frantic in my need to find the help that was beyond me. I found a women's bathroom and rushed inside, locking the door behind me. I leaned panting against it. Instantly a picture of Jaden from two days before flashed through my heart. I saw our curly-haired four-year-old sitting on the bathroom sink watching his daddy shave, his chubby fingers timidly touching the white foam on Kevin's face. My tears burst unchecked as I slumped against the white door. I understood for the first time that our son might not see his daddy shave again.

I cried out with tears pouring down my cheeks. "Please, Lord," I pleaded. "Don't take my husband. You took my mother when I was five. Don't take my children's daddy, too! Don't let him die!"

I wilted against the door, clinging to the shiny brass handle for support.

"Oh, Jesus, I don't know what to do!" I wailed. "I can't even think. Everything's all confused!"

My shoulders shook with the intensity of my tears. "Help me, Lord! Help me! I need You," I cried. "I need You!"

The unmistakable words of 2 Corinthians 12:9 broke clearly through my spinning mind: "My grace is sufficient for you, for My strength is made perfect in weakness" (NKJV).

A blanket of incredible peace began to gently envelop me, folding me inside, wrapping me in the strength that comes only through Jesus Christ. I felt like I had been picked up and was being held close in His arms. My thoughts began to focus as His strength wrapped around me. I leaned on Him with all there was of me. My sobs spent themselves, and my need began to be satiated. I could feel His presence. I savored His strength rising within me, and I knew I was not alone. The Savior was with me.

Another Scripture filled my mind, girding me like a brace. "All things work together for good to those who love God, to those who are the called according to His purpose" (Romans 8:28, NKJV). This was my ticket to trust Christ in all circumstances, and I grasped it with both hands like a child clutching a prize. I acknowledged Christ as Lord over every circumstance, and I anchored myself in Him. I knew that if Kevin died, God would bring good out of it and would carry me through every minute.

The peace in that moment was overwhelming. I felt calm and completely secure. I splashed cool water on my face at the sink, hardly noticing the red, swollen eyes reflected in the mirror or my blouse soaked with tears. I had come face-to-face with my human insufficiency, and I also had come face-to-face with the unlimited sufficiency of Christ. I recognized that I could never be enough because I had never been created to be enough, and He could never be limited. I was not caught by circumstances. I was caught in the arms of Christ. I felt focused and equipped to face what lay ahead. I walked out of the bathroom, gently closing the door behind me, ready to wait.

I was called to Kevin's bedside fifteen minutes later. He stirred when I took his hand. He opened his eyes to my face but immediately sank back into unconsciousness. Tubes and machines stood around him in sterile plastic wraps. Kevin's monitor, displaying new readings I did not understand, flashed rhythmically to the nurses' desk with his every breath. I sat quietly beside him, pouring my heart out to God. Armed by Christ, I prayed as a warrior fighting for Kevin's life.

Kevin's ICU nurse, Winnie, was a plump, blue-eyed woman with graying hair and a white uniform. Between the busyness of checking and connecting IV tubes, she chatted.

"Have you been in Richmond long?" She injected a vial into Kevin's IV.

I smiled wryly. "We got here last night."

"Do you have any children?" She added a new IV bag.

"Three," I replied. "A six-year-old girl, a four-year-old boy and a one-year-old boy."

Winnie paused from her work to look at me. Her light blue eyes squinted as she studied me. They were misty when she turned them away. She quietly left the room with her clipboard hanging limply at her side.

A little before ten o'clock, I was called from the ICU. The nurses' desk announced that I had visitors in the waiting room. I left reluctantly. I did not want to leave Kevin's side but I knew that the visitors could not enter the ICU.

I was greeted by three directors from the International Mission Board: the personnel director, the candidate director and the medical director. They were still wearing their suits and ties from the evening program. They hugged me in turn.

"Hello, Audra. How are you doing?" Dr. Atkinson, the personnel director, asked. He motioned me to a chair. "Is there anything we can get for you?"

I shook my head.

Dr. Williams, the medical director, asked, "Have you eaten dinner? Can we order a food tray or bring you something from outside?"

Again I shook my head. "No, thanks."

"Is there somebody we can call for you?" asked Dr. Riddle, the candidate director. "Does your family know how to reach you?"

"I'm okay," I assured them. "I've talked with our families, and they have the numbers to the ICU." I paused. "Everybody's in shock. We're all trying to figure out what happened."

I turned to Dr. Williams, a physician. He had been communicating with Kevin's doctor throughout the day. I had been told very little and had not seen Dr. Valdadoss since Kevin had been transferred to the ICU. I had been providing more answers to physicians than they had been giving to me. I asked Dr. Williams to explain Kevin's condition.

Dr. Williams cleared his throat. Choosing his words carefully, he gently described the seriousness of Kevin's illness. He explained that the lab tests had been inconclusive and that Kevin's disease was unknown, so the medical team was giving him a series of strong antibiotics in an attempt to cover several possibilities. Complicating matters, Kevin's blood platelets had fallen too low to continue more tests.

"Audra." Dr Williams cleared his throat again. "Kevin's body is shutting down. He's in septic shock and in DIC—organ failure, overcome by the apparent infection."

The men were grim-faced as Dr. Williams spoke. But their words were kind as they reassured me of their support. We joined hands and prayed for Kevin. The three men also prayed for me and our children at home.

I stood to return to the ICU. "God will bring good out of this," I told them. "He promised. No matter what happens, He will bring good for those who love Him, according to His purpose."

I stood resolutely before them, watching them slowly nod in agreement. Their eyes were moist as they looked at me. They promised their help in handling any details that might arise.

Dr. Riddle gave me his business card, writing telephone numbers on the back. "You can reach us at these numbers during the night. Don't hesitate to call if you need anything."

By midnight many friends and family members had called. Everyone struggled to comprehend what had happened. It seemed inconceivable. Kevin had always been healthy. No one understood how he could become gravely ill so suddenly. Those who telephoned called others into prayer. Friends and churches across the nation began to pray through the night on Kevin's behalf.

I continued to watch Kevin drift in and out of consciousness. His eyes would search for me when they opened, but I felt that at times Kevin did not recognize me. A surgeon inserted a Swan-Ganz catheter into his neck, and new readings emerged on his monitor. His body began to toss restlessly, jerking from one side to the other. Although he was opening his eyes more frequently, he seemed to be unaware of what he was doing. He did not seem to know that his body was tossing, nor did he seem able to control it. My attempts to soothe him failed.

"Mrs. Shelby, you have a phone call." The intercom buzzed from the nurses' station.

I pulled myself from Kevin's bedside to take the call at the nurses' desk. It was Dr. Valdadoss.

"Mrs. Shelby," he began. "Your husband is very sick. Has he taken any medications over the last few days? Has he been exposed to any illnesses that you know of?"

These were questions the doctor had asked before. Again I explained that before we left home Kevin had been fighting the onset of a cold. He had taken a decongestant, but that was the only medication I could remember. Again I explained that as a pharmaceutical sales rep he was frequently in and out of doctors' offices and could have been exposed to numerous illnesses. Again I said that Kevin had always been healthy.

Dr. Valdadoss struggled for words. He spoke disjointedly, pausing several times. He seemed to be searching for words, or not wanting to say the words he found.

"Mrs. Shelby, Kevin is very sick." He cleared his throat. "A healthy, fit man stronger and younger than Kevin would not be able to survive this kind of illness. Kevin doesn't have as much to fight with."

The doctor paused for a long couple of seconds. "Mrs. Shelby, we are doing everything we can. I will talk to you again in the morning." He clicked off the line.

I hung up the phone, puzzling over Dr. Valdadoss's words, trying to understand what he meant. And then I did. He was telling me my husband was going to die. Kevin had continued to deteriorate, and no one could determine the cause. He had received the strongest doses of the best medicines science could provide, but it wasn't enough. Kevin was not responding to treatment.

I sat down in the chair inside Kevin's room, no longer able to hold his hand because of the jerking of his body. His eyes opened but they no longer saw me. I strengthened my heart's grip on the Lord and cried out anew for Him to intervene and spare my husband's life.

At 3:30 in the morning, Winnie came to the door. "Mrs. Shelby, I'm sorry, but it's time for the shift change. You'll have to leave the ICU while the new shift does patient evaluations."

Winnie waited apologetically. "Get a soda from the machine and stretch your legs a bit. You haven't been out for a while—it'll do you good."

She gently nudged me out. "We'll call you if anything changes. It won't be for long." She walked with me to the ICU entrance and softly closed the door behind me.

I wandered through the quiet halls, praying as I walked. There was no activity in the ebbing of the night. A solitary man in a burgundy jumpsuit swabbed a mop back and forth across the floor of the silent corridor. Dim night-lights made dark waiting rooms appear gray and shrouded with shadows. They were still and quiet, silenced by departed visitors.

Remembering the peace God had given me earlier in the day, I looked for the bathroom where I had prayed. I wanted to return to it, but I had found it by wandering countless hallways. Now I could not find my way back. I searched two corridors and hesitated. I did not want to waste time or get farther from the ICU.

"Lord, where is it?" I stomped my foot in frustration. "It has to be here somewhere." I started to pivot when I noticed a brown door directly in front of me. It was labeled "Chapel" in big gold letters.

I chuckled. "Thanks, Lord."

The room was small and quiet, lined with yellow padded pews that faced a mahogany altar. A simple brass cross stood in the center of a linen altar cloth. Behind it was a stained-glass window illuminated with light. Feeling like I had been handed a gift, I walked quietly to the front and sat down.

I poured my heart out to God, pleading with Him to intervene. "Lord Jesus, all authority has been given to You. I ask in Your name that You spare Kevin's life."

With my face lifted upward, I prayed passionately and openly, free from human eyes, thinking of nothing except my husband and my need to have him spared. I could envision Kevin's jerking body, and my tears began to flow. My eyes were focused on the white ceiling as I cried my prayer upward.

Suddenly the ceiling began to change. It became like a flowing white curtain. I felt like I was standing at the footstool of Christ, like I was at His feet and He was standing just above the curtain in a place I could not see.

His words came clearly. "I have heard your prayer."

I stopped praying and blinked at the ceiling above me, not trusting my tear-filled eyes. In the fog of fatigue I was confused over what I had heard. Had I imagined the curtain that was no longer visible? Had I heard the voice of God, or was I imagining it? I sat still for a few moments, hesitant to believe and reluctant to leave, then I rose slowly from the pew.

"Lord, if You said You heard my prayer, I believe You. I know You can heal Kevin."

I made my way back to Kevin's room. I returned to my bedside vigil, praying as Kevin's body continued to toss from side to side. But as I watched, a change began to come over him. The tossing of his body began to slow. Eventually it stopped, and the jerking eased into an occasional turn to one side. Kevin settled into an almost passive sleep. I noticed on the monitor that his blood pressure rose slightly.

Cyndy, Kevin's morning nurse, noticed the change. She stood watching from the foot of his bed. A puzzled smile teased her mouth as she put her hand in the pocket of her paisley uniform.

"He is settling down," she announced. "I think he is doing better." She sounded surprised.

She walked to me and gently put her hand on my shoulder. "Mrs. Shelby, this would be a good time for you to get some rest. It will be okay if you leave him for a little while. He really is doing better."

She massaged my shoulders. "You need some sleep, honey. We'll get you if anything changes. I'll send a pillow and blanket to the waiting room. Go on, honey," she urged.

I watched Kevin, his body settling peacefully on the bed. I looked into Cyndy's kind, hazel eyes. I had slept less than three of the past 48 hours, and the strain of the day had taken its toll. But instead of feeling fatigued, I felt exhilarated.

"Thank you, Cyndy. Thank you!" I threw my arms around her neck, ecstatic that she confirmed what I saw happening. Kevin was better. The Lord had healed him.

On the afternoon of our eighth day at the hospital, Kevin was moved from the ICU to a private room for discharge the following day. I returned that evening to the hotel room that the International Mission Board had provided. I entered my dark room and tossed the car keys onto the desk. I started to close the drapes but stopped myself, caught by the bright light pouring from a nearby street lamp. It spilled through the window over the bed to the floor, marking a path like a river of light cutting through the darkness to guide me. I thought of Jesus pouring His light through the darkness of the previous days to light my way through them, and I knelt in that stream of light, tears flooding my cheeks. "Thank You, Jesus, for shining down on me," I wept. "Thank You for healing Kevin and letting us return home together to our children."

My bent knees did not feel adequate. My words did not feel enough. I wanted every part of me to praise God. I remembered David dancing before the Lord when the Ark of the Covenant returned to Jerusalem. I wanted to dance as David had, to move my body in passionate praise. I was saturated with joy in my Lord, who had answered my prayer and provided all I had needed.

In my hotel room, alone with my Savior, I danced with all of my might.

An early morning flight took us home the next day, six days later than our intended schedule. Kevin was pale and shaky and had lost twenty of his two hundred pounds, but he was alive. His medical team had included disease specialists from across the nation, but inconclusive tests had left them mystified. His illness remained undiagnosed.

Our return to life at home was joyful, but in our happy sunshine a gray cloud hovered. A friend commented that she had never seen walking death until she saw Kevin, who had been ruddy-faced and padded like a teddy bear but now appeared gaunt and frail. His green eyes big against his pale face, Kevin had little strength or energy and spent most of his time in his recliner, sleeping through the day and night.

Noise bothered Kevin, and he could tolerate little. The sounds of our active children irritated him and he struggled not to show it. He reached eagerly for their hugs but was relieved when they hurried away.

"Why can't Daddy read me a book, Mommy?" Madison asked, flipping the colorful pages in my lap. "Isn't Daddy all better now?" I assured her that he was.

Jaden could not understand why his daddy would not wrestle and play with him anymore. After Kevin brushed him aside again, Jaden yelled, "You're not my daddy!" and stomped his angry little feet down the hall to cry in his bedroom.

I seemed to constantly run interference between them all, wiping tears, handing out explanations, soothing hurt feelings. And I was tired. I tried not to complain; it made me feel ungrateful. I was elated that Kevin's life had been spared, but I wondered if God had spared his life but not his health. Kevin was not the husband or father he had been. I prayed for understanding and love for the one he had become.

The International Mission Board asked us to wait before rescheduling our Candidate Conference. I understood their hesitation. How could they approve us for appointment? Kevin had almost died from an unexplained illness. The possibility of its return lingered. Kevin remained optimistic, but watching his slow recovery, I wondered if his health would allow us to serve.

I tried to dance in the sunshine God had showered, but I felt like I was skipping under menacing thunderclouds that threatened gathering rain.

Two weeks after we returned home, Kevin began to run a low-grade fever. He blamed fatigue from returning to work, but I watched him closely. One night as Kevin got into bed, he winced. He shifted, unable to lie comfortably on his back without pain, and complained about a lump on his hip. It was hard, painful to the touch, warm and noticeably large.

"Kevin, you need to have that checked!" I exclaimed, setting aside the book I had been reading.

Kevin was in no hurry to see another physician. "I'm just tired," he answered. "I probably overdid it today. I'll be okay, sweetheart. It's nothing."

I folded my arms across my chest and sat cross-legged so that I could face him squarely on the bed. "What about that lump? What's that from?" I asked. "And your fever?"

"Probably from a shot in the hospital. I think I remember having a couple around there." He turned off his bedside lamp.

"They weren't that high on your hip, and they wouldn't make it swell like that." I got out of bed and switched on the overhead light. "Besides, you got most of your shots through your IV."

"Honey," Kevin sighed. "I'm fine. I'm just tired." He ran his hand through his thinning brown hair.

I walked to his side of the bed. "You ran a fever before, remember? Please have this checked out tomorrow!" I pleaded.

The next morning I read to the children and vacuumed the house more than it needed to be vacuumed as I waited for Kevin to call after his visit to the doctor.

He finally called at eleven. "Hi, sweetheart. I saw the doctor, and he thinks it's just fatigue after all that has happened." He cleared his throat. "He asked me to see a surgeon to make sure the lump isn't anything. I'm on my way there now."

I let out the breath I had been holding. "Good, I'm glad you're seeing the surgeon. How are you feeling?"

"Tired. A little cold, so my fever might have climbed, but I'll be okay. I'll be home in an hour or so."

Forty-five minutes later, the telephone rang. It was the surgeon, Dr. Wagoner. He spoke quickly.

"Mrs. Shelby? Your husband just left my office. He mentioned an injection he received, but he wasn't sure when. I have his hospital discharge summary, but he thought he received the shot a week before your trip to Virginia. Do you remember when he got it?"

"Yes," I answered. I knew Kevin had memory lapses during his illness and sometimes confused details. "It was the day before we left."

"Are you sure?" His urgency startled me.

"I'm positive," I answered slowly. "The kids ran up and hugged him when he got home from work. He yelped when their arms went around his hip."

I paused for a minute, remembering. "He said a doctor had given him a steroid shot to boost his immune system. The doctor was trying to help him ward off a cold since we were traveling the next day."

Dr. Wagoner's voice sprang from the phone. "I think that's it!" he exclaimed. "That shot is what did it! Listen," he added brusquely, "If his fever starts to spike, get him to the emergency room and I'll meet you there. It doesn't matter what time it is. Just get him to the hospital. Do you understand?"

I told him in a faltering voice that I understood and then tried to get the phone back into its cradle with my shaking hands. *We are going to go through this all over again*, I thought.

I hugged the children who had gathered around me. I prayed silently, fighting back tears. *Lord, please let Kevin be okay. Please let this all be over and Kevin be okay.*

Kevin spent the afternoon in his recliner, convincing me that he felt well. But when I returned from my evangelism course at church that night, Kevin met me at the door. His cheeks were flushed, and his eyes were glassy and bright.

"I don't feel so good," he mumbled, handing me Jack, who was asleep in his arms.

"I knew I shouldn't have gone," I wailed. "I knew I should have stayed home!" I threw my purse on the kitchen counter, put Jack in his crib and ran to get the thermometer.

Kevin's temperature was 101.5 and climbing. I felt like I had been handed a time bomb. I called my friend Ruth to stay with the kids, grabbed a duffel bag and started throwing in toothbrushes and pajamas.

Madison and Jaden watched me instead of their DVD. They said nothing, their blue eyes wide and frightened as I ran in and out of our bedroom.

I stopped to hug them. "I need to take Daddy to see the doctor." I tried to make my voice sound light. "We're going to get Daddy well once and for all."

We rushed to the hospital. At eleven o'clock Kevin was prepped and taken into surgery. Dr. Wagoner believed the lump was the site of an injection that had introduced an infection, still in his body. His plan was to clean out the site and remove the infected tissue. He came to me before he went into surgery.

"Mrs. Shelby." He paused. His green scrub hat was tight around his black hair, and his surgical mask dangled from his neck, waiting to be tied. "There is the possibility that the infection has spread into surrounding muscle," he said. "If so, we may have to do some grafts and reconstruction."

I nodded silently. He reached out and squeezed my arm. "I'll talk to you as soon as I can."

An hour and a half later, Dr. Wagoner appeared in the waiting room. I jumped from my seat, almost hitting the aquarium gurgling next to it.

"Kevin is going to be fine," he said, untying his scrub hat. "I removed a 175-gram mass of infected tissue from his hip. The wound is down to the muscle, but there was no damage to the muscle itself. It will need to heal from the inside out so it is packed, not sutured. The nurses will show you how to clean and repack it. Kevin will be fine."

I thanked him three times before he left, squeezing his hand repeatedly. Then I accompanied Kevin from recovery to his room and kissed his sleeping head.

"Thank You, Lord," I whispered. "Thank You."

Lab reports indicated that the tissue from Kevin's hip had been infected with staph aureus, confirming that the injection he had received from a multi-dose vial had been contaminated. The injection contained a colony of staph that had been sucked into the syringe and injected directly into Kevin's hip. Complicating the situation, the steroid, meant to be injected into the muscle, had been improperly injected into fatty tissue, outside of muscular blood circulation. The toxic serum had remained in the fatty tissue, preventing healing and hindering conclusive lab results in Virginia. A statistical analysis conducted by medical school residents rated the likelihood of this occurrence as a one in ten million possibility.

Eighteen months later we were on the plane bound for Yemen, and I thanked the Lord yet again as I watched my healthy husband sleeping in his seat. The cabin lights began to come on, and Madison and Jack stretched and yawned.

"We are about to land in Yemen! Can you see the lights outside the window?" My voice trembled with excitement. "That's Sana'a, our new home!"

The flight attendant walked down the aisle confirming that each seat belt was fastened. I pushed the button on my armrest to return my seat to its upright position and then clasped the children's hands tightly in my lap. I looked at the empty seats that the Hajj pilgrims had vacated for Mecca.

"You will be enough, Lord," I whispered. "When I forget, remind me. Give me glimpses of You."

The plane landed and then taxied to a stop at the gate. I helped the children gather their belongings and looked at Kevin. His eyes were shining as he grabbed his carry-on bag and took Jaden's hand.

I took a deep breath. *Okay, Lord. I'm ready.*

3

Reds, yellows, blues and greens splashed across the gray floor and into my sleeping eyes. Light and dark played on my face, teasing me awake. I blinked at the color and squinted to find its source. There was a stained-glass arch plastered high above each tall window of our bedroom.

I had not noticed them the night before. We had arrived at our new home at eleven o'clock in the Yemen night. We had unloaded luggage in a haze of fatigue, thanked our new colleagues for transporting us and then settled our sleeping children into their beds before falling fully clothed into our own.

Now as the late morning sun swabbed the floor with color, I nudged Kevin. "Are you awake?"

"Yeah." Kevin yawned, standing with me to stretch the stiffness from his muscles.

We padded barefoot down a wide green hall to the living room, where Madison and Jaden trudged sleepily to join us. Blue velour cushions bulged along the floor of two corner walls. This was the *mufraj*, our legless couch, and it received a prompt pounce from Madison and Jaden. Jack shuffled in, rubbing his eyes with one hand and tugging my wrinkled dress with his other. He squealed at the sight of furniture the height of his toddler legs and ran to bounce with his siblings.

A pine table and six chairs stood at the opposite end of the long room. I let out a sigh of relief. "I'm glad we have a table and chairs."

"What, you don't want to eat on the floor like the locals?" Kevin grinned, rubbing his stubbled chin.

"I do." I stifled my yawn. "But the kids need to learn table manners, too. They won't need help learning to eat off the floor."

"I'm hungwy!" Jack announced, straddling a mufraj cushion like a horse.

"Me, too!" echoed Madison and Jaden.

I yawned again and stood slowly from my armchair to stretch. "I'll see what's in the kitchen for breakfast."

I switched on a bare lightbulb dangling from a black cord. A fat, tan gecko rested high up on the white-plastered wall. On a pine cupboard countertop were cornflakes, tea bags, instant coffee and a clear plastic bag of coarse sugar. The biggest aluminum kettle I had ever seen swallowed the back of a small white stove. It was filled with water and labeled with a yellow sticky note, "Boiled." I poured water from it into a smaller kettle and struck a match to light an eye.

A banner with the crayoned words "Welcome to Yemen" decorated the white fridge. I smiled, stirring coffee into Kevin's cup and tea into mine, then put my spoon into a stainless steel sink. I looked beneath its blue-striped skirt at butane gas bottles hiding under the sink's lead pipe legs. I loaded the caffeine and cornflakes onto a melamine tray and carried it into the living room.

After breakfast Kevin and I sorted through suitcases for clean clothes while the children scrounged for their toys. None of us had bathed for three days, and although the children would be content to continue without, Kevin and I were desperate for hot showers. I was grateful for the hot water heater in our one large bathroom. I was more grateful, however, for the pink toilet that sat next to the pink bathtub. While the bathroom did house one of the holes dubbed "squatty potties" by foreigners, we were blessed to have a *kursi feransi,* or "French chair," as the locals called the toilet.

Showered and clean, I sorted clothes into tall pine wardrobes, musing over the lack of built-in closets. I noticed the children staring through the doorway.

"Mommy," Madison asked hesitantly. "Can we go outside and play?"

"Great idea! Kevin!" I called him away from untangling computer cords.

We filed from our wide front porch into a yard of dirt, gravel and a scraggly patch of grass guarded by a small tree. Jaden was immediately up the tree, calling for Madison to join him.

I studied the tree. It appeared strong. Small and wiry, its branches seemed sturdy. "Do you think it's strong enough to hold them?" I asked Kevin.

Kevin studied the tree. "Probably."

The high concrete block walls surrounding our yard were dotted with shrubs of bougainvillea. The front wall was covered by jasmine with vines overhanging the street. Our house looked like a flat gingerbread house. Built with the warm brown of mud bricks, its windows and roof edges were outlined with white paint, like iced gables on gingerbread. It was only one story, however, which seemed to be the exception in our neighborhood. Surrounding houses had the same mud bricks and white-traced windows, but they stood three stories high, towering above our walls. I ran my hand over my uncovered hair. Because the neighbors could easily see into our yard, I would need to wear a scarf even here.

I looked up at the neighboring windows. I was eager to meet the women I knew were inside. I had plans to share Christ, and I was ready to get started, even if it was against Yemeni law.

"I'll start with my language tutor next week," I said aloud. I hoped she would be as eager to hear as I was to share. I swallowed. *Lord, help me to be effective,* I prayed. *Use me to tell her the truth about You.*

"Mommy," Madison yelled from the red flowers she was picking. "Jack's going to the bathroom outside!"

I spun around to see Jack's small white bottom bared as he calmly watered the gravel.

"Jack, baby, no!" I shouted, knowing it was too late to stop him but wanting to anyway. "We use the potty inside!" My eyes shot to the tall windows of the houses overlooking our yard. I wondered how many of our neighbors were watching.

Kevin came up beside me. "See how fast our children are adapting to the local culture?" He grinned.

"Ha, ha," I retorted. "I suppose you'll be next? I hear the men do it outside, too, even on the street."

Kevin's response was lost as the cry of prayer calls began to blare from countless minarets interspersed throughout the city. They rang out sequentially, a thousand loudspeaker voices wailing one second after the other. The cry was lyrical and haunting, yet resolute. Jack grabbed both my legs and buried his head in my skirt. He pulled me to hold him. Madison jumped from her flowers and Jaden from the rocks he was sorting. Their hands were poised, their eyes gripping mine, as they stood ready to bolt toward me. Kevin looked at his watch. It was half past noon.

"It's all right, guys. It's just the prayer call. Let's go inside and find some lunch." I picked up Jack.

Madison and Jaden followed Kevin. Roasting garlic and simmering spices I had not yet met lassoed me from a neighboring kitchen. We all paused, sniffing the air. "I wonder what our neighbors are cooking for lunch," I said. Jaden asked me to cook whatever they were cooking.

"Yuck." Madison wrinkled her nose and shook her head as the smells intermingled with an indiscriminate puff of raw sewage.

✦

We began language study the week after our arrival. Kevin studied Arabic for three hours each day on our mufraj with Mohammed, a thin young man who spoke passable English. Jaden and Jack played at home and challenged Rose, our Ethiopian housekeeper, for entrance into Kevin's Arabic lesson. Madison began the last quarter of second grade at an English-speaking school.

I was to study the same language curriculum with my tutor, Fatima. I left for her apartment that first morning dressed appropriately. I covered my head with a huge scarf, although I did not enjoy it, nor did I enjoy the way my hair looked when I was later free to uncover it. I wore a loose-fitting dress with trousers underneath to cover my legs and thought how eager I was for our crates to arrive with my blue jeans and polo shirts to wear inside the privacy of our home.

I walked the mile and a half to Fatima's apartment. The streets were full of taxis and obnoxious drivers, and fares were cheap, but I preferred the walk. I loved listening to the voices I passed. Men in ankle-length tunics belted with curved daggers talked with other men dressed the same way, the shoulders of their dark blue blazers draped with red or black checked prayer shawls. Other men hurried past in muted plaid shirts and gabardine trousers with briefcases tucked under their arms. Yet the voices that intrigued me most were those of the women who walked hand-in-hand with children or in clusters of other women shrouded in black. They talked and chuckled together, were silent to the men they passed but grew loud when they challenged the shopkeepers for a bargain. They were like jewels draped by their religion but sparkling with life underneath.

I want to know them, Lord, I prayed as I passed a group of three. *Help me get beyond their veils to show them who You are.* I thought of Fatima and the many lessons ahead of us. I swallowed. *Will I be able to show Fatima, Lord? To tell her about You?*

I threaded my way through streets congested with traffic. Rattling taxis bobbed around dusty SUVs. Military jeeps, jutting with machine guns and soldiers, forced their lead in front of dark sedans. Donkey carts and motorcycles jostled for place between minivans and trucks. It seemed that each driver vied to be first and unhesitatingly created six lanes where two had been marked.

The first time I had to cross one of those swarming streets I was bewildered. *How am I going to cross this intersection, Lord?* I stared at the thicket of cars. I made feeble attempts to navigate across, but each time I drew back. Then I watched the locals. They forded a channel boldly through, stretching out their hands in a gesture like holding a pinch of cotton. I did the same and boldly rode the wake behind them.

As I reached the other side I gasped. "Oh, my!" A wiry old man herding his flock of goats and sheep faced me on the sidewalk. I moved aside to let him pass. Unmindful of my gawking eyes, he paused at an overfilled Dumpster and raked piles of garbage back onto the street. He prodded his animals to forage through the refuse, then herded them on with his stick, leaving behind what the herd left behind.

"No wonder there is garbage everywhere," I muttered, side-stepping rotten banana peels.

I passed a housewares store and stepped carefully between towers of aluminum pans stacked on the sidewalk. Grains bulged in open burlap bags at the shop next door. I fingered roots and sniffed spices and incense pebbles protruding from a drawer.

"Welcome, welcome!" A man appeared from his stool and waved me to enter.

I jumped, feeling caught and obligated to make a purchase. I stumbled through Arabic to buy a half-kilo of bulgur I already had at home.

In a dusty alley I dodged boys racing after tin cans they propelled with sticks. Other boys waited for cars to pass so they could kick a deflated soccer ball to a rock-and-stick goalpost. I approached a doorstep where little girls in embroidered leggings leaned on bigger girls wearing white head scarves. Some of the girls smiled shyly back from their perch on the steps. Others stared as I walked past. A girl about four years old ran up to me to get a better look, standing just inches away.

Almost to Fatima's house I was met by two smiling girls who looked about seven or eight. Their dark curls were tied in unmatched ribbons and their blue school uniforms were brushed over with dust, as were their once-white socks.

"Thank you, thank you," they greeted me in accented English.

I was confused. I did not know whether to answer, "You're welcome," or to explain what they were saying, or to teach them "Good morning." I finally gave each girl a piece of wrapped candy and said *ma'a salama* [good-bye]. After that the little girls met me each morning, and I kept candy in my pockets.

Fatima greeted me with a kiss on one cheek and then the other as she clasped my hand in traditional greeting. "*Asalam alaykum* [Peace be upon you]," she said.

Fatima was fifteen years my junior and did not know it. She related to me as a peer. It was not that I looked young for my age; it was that the Yemeni women my age appeared much older, so Fatima did not see me as 39. Fatima was lovely with wavy black hair, large brown eyes and an Arab nose that began high and curved down over her full lips. She had a manner that was both transparent and secretive, faltering and arrogant, all at the same time.

Fatima read her Quran and said her five prayers at home each day. She wore her black *balto* cloak whenever she went out in public and covered her hair without exception around any man that was not her husband, father or brothers. But like other southern Yemeni women, Fatima did not veil her face, a practice for which she was ridiculed by local northern women, who veiled their faces.

I soon learned that northern women considered southern women to be less pious and devout than they and treated their southern counterparts with disdain and criticism, a residue of civil war propaganda. I had known that Yemen had once been two countries that had combined into one in 1990 and unified after a civil war in 1994. But I had not known that the victorious agricultural north continued to disdain the technological and defeated south, perhaps a reflection of reverse treatment prior to the war.

Her hair hidden under a thin, orange scarf, Fatima invited me into her upstairs apartment. She pulled me away from the curious eyes of her neighbor, who was also her landlady and appeared in the hall when she heard my footsteps on the stairs. Her neighbor was a northern woman who could be both pleasant and hostile within the same conversation. Inside closed doors, Fatima relaxed her head scarf. "*Marhaba* [Welcome]," she said, waiting as I placed my white athletic shoes, layered brown with Sanaani dust, on the shoe rack next to her painfully high black vinyl heels.

She led me past her bare kitchen with its lonely fixtures: a small stove and a meager assortment of dishes drying on a steel sink drain board. Her bedroom was across from it, a room dwarfed by a pine bed and matching wardrobe furnished by her husband in their marriage agreement. Her one bathroom was sunny and clean and kept meticulously closed to keep contained the naughty *jinns* [spirits] that were believed to live inside.

We sat on the thin, beige-sheeted pad that served as her mufraj. The room's two windows were curtained with tan, flowered sheets. A ceramic vase of red plastic flowers sat on a corner shelf. We leaned against the yellow painted wall and began studying Arabic words for food and shopping.

When we finished, Fatima served hot, sweet tea spiced with cardamom, cinnamon and milk, along with a dish of cream-filled cookies. "Eat, Audra. Take your rest," she urged. This became our ritual.

Fatima served refreshments every time I entered her house. If she had none to serve, she would send the neighbor's children to the shop across the alley to purchase some. She modeled the Arab law of hospitality, teaching me that every guest must be served refreshment. I had to learn not to model the American law of personal preference. I despised cream-filled cookies. I flinched every time I saw her tray. But I learned to smile as I ate them.

Fatima was hungry for companionship. A new bride recently pregnant, she spoke some English and discussed everything with me—except Jesus. She would not let me talk about Him.

One afternoon we were chatting as we sipped our tea.

"Audra," Fatima began cautiously, leaning back against the wall and hugging a pillow to her abdomen. "In America do mothers treat their sons' wives badly?"

"Not usually. In some homes maybe," I answered. "My mother-in-law is like my own mother. She treats me like one of her daughters."

"Hmmph." Fatima snorted. "My mother-in-law has a black heart. She treats me like *khidama* [a servant]. Before I married her son, she invited me to her home and gave a party for me. She was good to me. But now I am khidama to her. What kind of aunt is this? Why does she do this?"

I sat forward from my slump against the wall. "Aunt?" I asked, surprised.

"Yes, of course, my *ama*, my father's sister." She was surprised by my surprise.

"Your husband is your first cousin?" I asked.

"Of course." She frowned. "Why are you asking me this? It is better to marry the son of an aunt or uncle so a bride will know the kind of man her husband is. He will be from her family."

"Ah," I nodded, understanding. Before marriage, a Yemeni bride knew her husband by appearance only. Most contact was forbidden. A bride could not know what her husband was like beyond his appearance. If he was a close relative, the bride had the perceived security of family connections to protect her.

The midday prayer call wailed out from the mosque down the block. I stood to go as Fatima pulled out her prayer rug and pointed it east toward Mecca. Fatima motioned me to sit back down.

"Wait, Audra. *Glissee* [sit]. I will be finished soon."

I sat down. I was curious but hesitant to watch her prayers. Fatima put on flip-flops to enter her closed bathroom.

"Fatima, I can't stay long." I looked at my watch. "I need to fix lunch for my family." Fatima did not answer. I remembered that it was forbidden to talk in the bathroom in the vicinity of lurking jinns.

Fatima returned from washing her face, arms and feet. With her limbs partially dabbed dry, she stood at the edge of her prayer rug. She smiled briefly and knelt, turning her face to greet the angels she believed were sitting on each of her shoulders. She bowed her face to the floor and began to recite her prayer. She extended her arms with her palms upward. Her lips moved in whispers. She lowered her head occasionally to touch the floor.

I wanted to leave. I wished I had not stayed. I felt like her prayer was a demonstration not to confirm her piety but to convert me to it. I turned my face and counted the rings on the curtain rod. I wondered what Madison was doing and if the boys had made it into Kevin's Arabic lesson. A flicker of anger pricked me inside.

When she finished Fatima stood slowly and rolled up her rug. A calm, pleased look spread over her face. She sat down on the thin foam mufraj and picked up the Quran I was not allowed to touch.

"Audra, do you pray?" She lifted her chin high and arched her eyebrows at me.

"Of course I pray," I answered. I wanted to add, "but not as a show for others."

"How many times?" Her tone sounded more accusing than curious.

"Our Book says that we are to pray all the time, without ceasing," I answered. "There are certain times I pray— before I eat to thank God for food and at night with my children to thank Him for the day. I pray early in the morning when I am alone with God and study His Book. But I also pray when I am walking in the street or cooking or anytime."

She frowned as she digested my words. "But how do you wash before you pray?" she asked. "How can you pray all the time when you must be clean before the God to pray?"

"Fatima," I answered. "Being clean before God is more than washing the outside of your body. How can God be satisfied with somebody that is clean on the outside if her heart is unclean on the inside?"

Fatima did not hesitate. "Our prayers and good deeds make us clean on the inside."

"Prayers and good deeds are strong enough to change one's heart?" I challenged. "How can they be? If you hate someone in your heart but you do good deeds, has the hate in your heart changed?"

Fatima knew I knew her feelings for her mother-in-law. She shrugged. "It is enough."

"How do you know it is enough, Fatima?" I continued. "God does not think as a man thinks. How do you know this makes you clean enough for God?"

"How can anyone know this, Audra?" Fatima answered. She set aside her Quran and sighed deeply as she collected our teacups on her plastic tray. She leaned back again and sat silent for several minutes.

"The God is merciful," she said slowly, shrugging her thin shoulders. "One can only hope for His mercy." She glanced at her Quran and sighed again.

"Fatima, God requires perfection. No matter how merciful He is, He requires us to be perfect."

Fatima nodded vigorously in agreement, almost upsetting the tea tray. "Yes, yes, of course." She seemed pleased to find something we both believed.

"But," I kept talking. "We cannot be perfect on the outside and imperfect on the inside. That is not perfection. It is an appearance. It only looks like perfection."

I moved closer to her on the mufraj. "We can never be as perfect as God requires, Fatima. How could we? It is beyond our ability. That is why God Himself provided the only Way we could be made perfect before Him. He provided the Perfect One, Jesus, the Messiah."

The minute I spoke Jesus' name Fatima's chin jerked up, and she turned her face away, standing immediately with her tray. "It is late," she said. "My husband will be home for his lunch."

She waited for me to gather my things. I sighed and put my notebook and pen into my bag. I had mentioned Jesus; our conversation was over. I looked at Fatima. She had told me what she believed about Jesus. He was the Isa of the Quran: an important prophet who had never sinned, had healed the sick and had raised people from the dead. But she believed Him to be a lesser prophet than Mohammed. She told me what she believed, but she would not allow me to tell her what I believed. It was almost as if she was afraid.

I closed my bag and followed her from the living room. I kissed both of her cheeks before slipping into my shoes.

"Ma'a salama," I whispered.

"Ma'a salama. *Hata bukrah.* [Good-bye. Until tomorrow.]" She hugged me, searching my face to see if she had offended me. She pressed a cream cookie into my hand to eat on the way home. She peered through the crack in her door as it closed between us.

I walked slowly down the steps and into the dirty alley, kicking a stone along the dry, dusty ground. I had never met anyone so convinced that what I believed was wrong, and who believed so strongly in what I knew to be wrong.

The sun burned through my dark jumper and scorched the street under my stinging feet. There was no shade along the sidewalk.

I wondered why Fatima believed the Bible was corrupt. Because she had been taught that from birth? I kicked away a candy wrapper that had blown against my shin. A new question wormed its way into my thoughts. Would I believe the Quran if I had been taught it instead of the Bible?

My head was sweating under my scarf. The sun seemed to bore right through it. I loosened it, wishing I had not bought the bulgur. I had one hundred riyalls left in my purse, enough for either cold bottled water or a ride home, and I wanted both. My throat was parched and stinging from blowing grit. I flagged a taxi and murmured directions in Arabic. I would wait to drink the pure water I knew was at home.

The high altitude sky poured unfiltered sun across the city. It was Thursday, the end of the Yemeni week, like Saturdays in America. Friday is the Islamic day of worship, and that was the day we met with other Christian foreigners for worship in a private apartment compound. But Thursdays were ours as a family.

We walked hand-in-hand down cracked, sporadic sidewalks, maneuvering Jack in a borrowed umbrella stroller between Madison and Jaden. Kevin returned the greetings of men we passed and stopped to talk with one who stopped to talk with him. The man laughed outright at Kevin's attempts to speak Arabic. Kevin grinned a lopsided smile and mispronounced the words again.

"This is good you speak Arabic!" the man said, his cheek bulging like a tennis ball with his wad of *qat* inside. He slapped Kevin twice on the back and went on his way chuckling.

We were accustomed to the laughs and bulging cheeks of qat-chewing men. But the mildly narcotic leaf made it difficult to understand their Arabic. Words were slurred, and we were distracted by the green juice trickling through their teeth.

We passed a fabric shop, and I stopped. "Honey, I need to buy fabric for that wedding I'm supposed to go to with Fatima. She was very particular about what to wear."

Kevin grimaced. "Do we have to get it now? You know how I love going into fabric stores."

I laughed. "I'll be quick. Besides, the clerks are all men. You can practice your Arabic. Madison, can you help me find something pretty and shiny?"

I spotted a bolt of navy blue chiffon. Madison fingered its gold metallic embroidery. "You'll look like a princess, Mommy."

"This good for wedding," the man assured me as he slit three meters from the bolt.

I grinned at Kevin. "Now I have to figure out how to make a *dera*."

"Dera?" A woman turned from the bolt of orange silk she was contemplating. She took my chiffon and folded it lengthwise. "Cut a hole here for neck." She pointed to the center of the fold. "Sew sides but not here. Here holes for arms."

I took the chiffon as I searched her veiled face. "*Shukran katheer* [Thank you very much]!" I exclaimed.

Her kind brown eyes nodded through her veil.

I followed Kevin out with the children, turning back to look at the woman. She and the shopkeeper had begun negotiating the price of the orange silk.

We continued our trek, passing other shops staffed by men. Even wooden carts selling women's undergarments were staffed by qat-chewing male vendors. They hawked lacy, sensual underwear openly and loudly to fully veiled, black-garbed and gloved women. I stopped to watch. These shrouded women kept their eyes downcast and their demeanor quiet to other men. They displayed every appearance of modesty. But they haggled sharply and none too discreetly with male vendors over satin bras and bright bikini panties.

I listened. A woman began her bargain with *bismillah* [in God's name], a word mutually spoken to invoke God's blessing. Then frilly underwear passed back and forth between gloved fingers and bare male hands as both squabbled over prices. Kevin nudged me to move on, but I could not. I wanted to see if the woman would win her price and leave with the underwear.

Jaden pulled my arm. "Mommy, come on!"

I sighed. The bargaining was still in progress, but I let myself be pulled back to resume our pace on the sidewalk. I moved closer to Kevin. "I'd wear a veil, too, if I had to bargain for my underwear from a man on a busy street."

Kevin laughed.

I whispered again, "Did you hear them say 'bismillah'? They use God's name in everything."

A few weeks later on the day of the wedding I was to attend with Fatima, the telephone interrupted our breakfast. Kevin talked with the voice on the other end and grinned as he hung up the phone. "We've been here two months, and our crates have been shipped, just like they said," he reported. "They left Houston last week. Should be here the first week of September."

"Hallelujah!" I yelled. "Blue jeans and my own pots and pans! Christian books! In English!"

Then I chewed my lip, thinking. I did not want them to arrive the first week of September. That would be the week before Madison and Jaden started school. I did not want the children to see the Christmas presents we had packed in the crates.

I thought about the problem as I waited for a taxi to Fatima's house. I ducked into a secluded corner.

Lord, I prayed, *could You bring in our crates the week after school starts? With the kids back in school, it sure would make things easier.* Then I climbed into the taxi and headed to Fatima's house for the wedding.

I waited thirty minutes for Fatima in her living room. I was wearing the dera I had made, with a gold satin sash tied around my waist. I had fixed my hair with mousse, as Fatima had instructed, and layered on more makeup than I had worn in a decade.

Fatima finally appeared, breathlessly stuffing things into a plastic sack as she snapped her balto cloak down over her pregnant abdomen.

"Sorry, Audra. The three days of the wedding are quite busy. We must go now, *besurah* [quickly]. We are late."

"Three days?" I asked.

"Yes. You do not remember the three days of the wedding?" She wrapped her black *hejab* [head covering] tightly around her hair. "The blue day, the green day and the white day?"

"No." I tried to keep pace with her as we walked down the alley. Fatima motioned for a taxi and gave directions to the driver. We climbed into the backseat.

"There are three days for a wedding," Fatima explained quietly in English. "Sometimes four, two if the groom has little money. Each day there is a feast and the bride wears a dress in a special color like blue or green. She wears her gold jewelry from the marriage agreement. The last day she wears a white dress like you wear in America. It is the day she goes to her husband's house."

We stopped at a beige, three-story building with tan curlicues around the windows. I paid the price Fatima negotiated with the driver, and we entered the iron gate. The courtyard was empty, spaced with plantless oval holes and a stairwell leading to each level of the multi-family dwelling. The bride and her family lived at the bottom. We made our way to their door.

At the second doorbell ring, one of the bride's sisters cautiously peered through the crack she opened. Reassured that we were women, she pulled us in with hugs and kisses, clutching her unbuttoned duster closely. Her copper-streaked black hair was crowned with fat pink curlers. I could hear a hair dryer buzzing in the background.

Huda, the bride's mother, hurried to gush a welcome as she led us to an open bedroom. She had fine graying hair, worried brown eyes and a plump bosom that overflowed her faded housedress. She appeared to be my age.

Four girls were in the bedroom, all twenty years old and younger. They were clustered around a bed strewn with lipsticks, eyeliners, rouges and assorted kegs of eye shadow. In the center, with her knees folded on the bed, was the bride, a girl of seventeen or eighteen. Hovering over her was the *coiffeura,* wielding a round hairbrush and a hot hair dryer like they were weapons. I winced as the young beautician tugged each bridal lock into place. The bride did not seem to notice. She sat placidly as her curls were sprayed solidly into place with two bottles of hair spray.

When the hair was finished, the beautician applied the bride's makeup. Eye shadow in three shades of lavender was followed by black eyeliner and a heavy coating of mascara. Then the bride's neck and face was sponged profusely with pale beige makeup and powder to lighten her olive skin. I smiled as I thought of American brides in tanning booths before their weddings.

After the bride's cheeks were shined with rouge and her lips lined and filled with maroon lipstick, she was presented to a mirror on the side of a double wardrobe, the only other furnishing in the large room. The girls praised her fine appearance. The bride studied her face from side to side but said nothing. She was wordlessly led to another room to be dressed by her mother and aunts in her full-length white gown.

I watched her as she left. She seemed neither happy nor sad, neither excited nor bored. She was almost expressionless. I wondered what she was thinking as she was being adorned to meet her husband. I wondered how she felt about leaving her father's dominion for her husband's.

After the bride left, the beautician turned to the other young women, who were eager for their turns. *"Ta'allee* [come]," she invited.

These girls were unmarried and not permitted to wear makeup, perfume or fancy curls. But weddings were exceptions. I looked at Fatima. She was as eager for the makeover as the others.

One by one the coiffeura fashioned the girls into the beauties of Arab folklore. I was awed by the transformation. Where they had been shy and giggling and nudging each other, they emerged confident and independent, even disdainful. Their painted appearance seemed to change their personalities. I was surprised by the difference.

The beautician motioned for me to sit, inviting my turn with her raised hairbrush and makeup applicators. I smiled.

"Lah, shukran [No, thank you]," I said, keeping my eyes off the thick wads of greased hair and dirt that filled her unwashed brushes. I went to the wardrobe mirror and applied my own red lipstick, straightening my sash and fluffing out my hair. Fatima preened beside me.

"Gamila [Beautiful]!" I told her. The other girls agreed.

We admired each other, and after several minutes we moved to the long mufraj room that would house the celebration.

"Where are the groom and his guests?" I asked Fatima as we settled down on plump black cushions.

"At his father's house several miles from here. Many men will gather there. They will chew qat and listen to music."

I nodded. I had heard weddings in my neighborhood. Boys sang responses as an entertainer crooned Islamic choruses to the sounds of a strumming *oud* and the banging of a large tin pan.

"Where will the wedding ceremony be?" I asked.

"The groom, his father and the bride's father will go to the mosque and make the marriage. Then they will come for the bride and take her to her husband's home."

Fatima chuckled. "There will be much noise. They will sound the horns the whole way to the bride and also when they take her home. They will come in cars covered with ribbons."

"You mean the bride doesn't attend her own wedding ceremony?" I was astonished.

"At the mosque with men?" Fatima laughed. "*Mush momken* [not possible]. Her father is there. That is enough." She shrugged. "They will come for the bride when it is over."

I leaned back against my cushions, thinking about the bride's expressionless face. *Would it be enough?* I wondered.

The carpet had been removed, leaving bare a skinny strip of tiled floor for dancing. I watched Fatima as she talked with her friends. She had become an exotic beauty, her black hair billowing around her kohl-lined eyes and pale powdered cheeks. She wore a flowing pink gown, heavily embroidered in silver and gold across her bulging middle. She held her head high, like a princess holding court. I felt proud of her, grateful for her opportunity to look and feel beautiful.

Women began to arrive in the entry hall, peeling away their black outer coverings. I watched in amazement as shimmering bodies emerged from the black shrouds. One woman sparkled in a purple silk caftan, her arms gleaming with gold jewelry. Two girls in their twenties removed *sirwal* pants to tug sequined miniskirts into place on their thighs. They ignored the disapproving frowns of two older women in rose and yellow silk deras, as did a girl in a red spaghetti-strapped dress who constantly tugged at her bodice.

One by one they emerged from their heavy black drapes. I smiled to myself. *If people only knew what was under those veils.* I realized that a woman could wear what she wanted under a covering as long as her appearance to the public was devout and pious.

I looked at their faces, artfully painted with makeup. I wished Kevin could see how beautiful they were. He knew them only as they appeared in public: dark eyes in narrow black slits.

I noticed Fatima and two friends whispering together on the mufraj. They were all looking at me.

"She is a *mussihiya* [Christian]?" The girl's surprise had raised her voice.

Fatima nodded, arching her eyebrows at me and folding her arms across her chest. All three girls stared at me with equally lofty eyebrows. They straightened their backs and lifted their heads. They seemed higher as they looked down on me.

One girl's smile turned to a sneer. "Mussihiya," she repeated.

The other girl seemed perplexed and agitated. "But she is friendly and nice. She is *habooba* [lovely]!" Her bewildered whisper was loud in the room. I smiled appreciation at her, but my smile faded at the other girl's haughty eyes.

That girl leaned closer. "Islam is *hallee* [sweet]," she said loudly.

Conversations between the women around us grew silent. They nodded their heads vigorously in agreement and focused on me, waiting collectively for my response. I looked to Fatima, but she was waiting with them. I grappled for words and wrestled with pride. I had never before been treated as inferior because of my faith and nationality, especially by the people of an impoverished country.

Lord, help! I prayed inwardly.

Out loud I slowly responded, "The way of Jesus is sweet. It is enough for me. Jesus is all that I need to walk with God."

"*Ma'a sha'allah* [What God wills]," one woman whispered.

The girl protested. "But we have *Isa* [Islamic name for Jesus] in our Quran. He is one of our prophets."

She was interrupted as two of the bride's sisters entered the room carrying trays of perfume. The women turned from me to the perfumes, eager to spray their necks, arms and dress fronts. The room had grown crowded, and the smell of perspiration had risen with the heat. Now heavy perfume saturated the air, intended to cover unpleasant odors.

I squelched my urge to cough and sneeze as my eyes watered. When the tray reached me, I declined the heavy dousing. I had spritzed myself earlier with a quiet, feminine scent. I did not see it among the ornate bottles on the tray.

Fatima touched my arm, her eyes full of concern. "You must wear perfume for your husband, Audra. It will please him, and he will love you."

"I am already wearing perfume," I answered.

Fatima leaned closer to sniff. "It is not enough. Here, you must wear these." She handed me a little red bottle and a large purple one. "Yours is not strong enough."

I did not want more perfume. I knew what Kevin's reaction would be. It would not be *amore*. He would wrinkle his nose, hold me at arm's length and push me toward the shower. But I sighed and turned my neck to let Fatima spray one scent after the other.

A woman I had met at Fatima's house came over to greet me. She kissed my hand in a tradition I quickly learned to repeat. Holding my right hand in hers, she kissed it and with her hand thrust it back to me. I kissed her hand and she pulled it back to kiss mine again. When she had both given and received adequate kisses, she smoothed her pink dera to sit beside me. Her neck was heavily laced with gold chains. A circle of jasmine buds was pinned around her curly black hair.

"Intee Amrekia? Kaif al Yemen? [You are an American? How (do you like) Yemen?]" A gold crown flashed on a front tooth.

"Hallo gidan [Very nice]," I answered.

She asked me how many children I had, and I answered, but then her next question confused me. I thought I had misunderstood, and I turned to Fatima for help.

Fatima quickly translated, "What kind of birth control do you use?" and turned back to her own conversation.

I sat silent, staring at the woman's kohl-lined eyes. I tried to smile. I leaned back to Fatima and whispered in English, "Do you really talk about such things with strangers?"

Irritated by my repeated interruption, Fatima responded sharply, "Of course, why not?" She turned her back to me and resumed her conversation.

I thought over the rules of conversation Fatima had taught me. I was not to discuss politics, wars or any unpleasant subject while visiting women. Those were considered men's issues and bad manners for women. I chewed on the inside of my lip, struggling with my own definition of bad manners.

Tired of waiting, the woman moved to a new line of questions. "Where does your husband work? What is his salary? What do you pay for your house?"

I straightened my dress and adjusted my legs to mask my discomfort. I feigned a lack of comprehension, stumbling around in Arabic to avoid answering. I was spared when two girls entered the room with a large CD player. The women began to clap, and I sighed with relief as rhythmic male crooning poured into the room.

Two teenage girls stepped into the narrow strip of floor as the rest of the crowd clapped and yelled. One of the girls tied her long black hejab [head scarf] around her hips as a sash and faced the other girl from the opposite end of the floor. Both began to shimmy and step toward each other with the music, their hips shaking and their arms and hands moving in rhythm.

I was amazed. I had never seen such a beautiful harmony of hips, hands and feet. I could not keep from gawking. Girls as young as ten began to dance and swivel their hips with amazing skill, shaking things I did not know could be shaken. In pairs, girl after girl, woman after woman sashayed across the floor as others clapped and yelled a high-pitched, curdling trill.

Then one young woman danced up to me and pulled my arms to join her. I pulled back, shaking my head with an emphatic *no*. I wanted to learn each fascinating step, but I wanted to learn them in front of the mirror on my closed bedroom door. The girl would not accept my refusal. She continued to pull me up to dance.

When I reluctantly stood, a sea of clapping erupted. The women called out encouragement, trilling me forward. I moved my gold sash from my waist to my hips, wondering if I could make it sway at all. I swallowed and took my place on the floor, closing my eyes as the music played.

I stepped to the music, feeling like my hands had become my feet and my hips had become immobile. I curled my wrists in and out as I tried to sashay, wondering if everything was moving at the same time but not daring to look. Painfully I made it across the floor, grateful when I reached my partner and the dance ended.

Applause thundered from the crowd of women around me. I was startled by it but smiled my appreciation as I sat down, my cheeks flaming. I mopped my sweaty forehead and neck with the handfuls of tissues that had been instantly offered. I looked around at the women. They were beaming at me. I realized they were pleased more by my willingness to dance with them than they were by my skills in dancing. I smiled back at the faces smiling at me. I felt like I had danced over the threshold and into their lives.

We continued to wait for the bride. I fanned myself with a flimsy square of pink tissue. More women had squeezed into the room. Younger girls were shuffled off the mufraj to the floor. I guessed there to be seventy bodies in a room built for thirty. *Kirkadey*, a dark red drink made from hibiscus leaves, was served around the room by the bride's mother. I downed my small glass and set it back on the tray to be refilled for others.

Sweat trickled down my chest. The heavy scent of perfume no longer lingered. It had failed to mask the odor of hot, sweaty bodies. I looked longingly at the four tall windows behind me. They were latched tightly closed to shut out the danger of peeping males. Water beaded on the glass, dripping down in rivulets. I fanned myself faster and tried not to think about the fresh breeze that had also been shut out. I turned my eyes away.

For the first time I noticed the dancers were all girls and women under thirty. Women my age and older were seated on cots in the outer reception hall. They seemed disinterested in the dancing. They shared apple-spiced tobacco in a water pipe and chewed skimpy leaves of qat while talking about the eight or nine children they had birthed and the years of hard work they had survived. I looked around at the young women dancing and chatting in the crowded room. I wondered if they would one day sit with water pipes and chew leftover qat in outer halls.

The room had grown hotter. Boxes of tissues were passed around again, and each woman took several to dab her face and neck. I was honored as a foreign guest and offered a lone bottle of water, which I promptly shared with Fatima. I looked at my watch. It was after eight o'clock. We had been waiting three hours for the bride.

"Fatima," I touched her arm. "You must not get too hot. It is not good for the baby." I patted her bulging abdomen. "You should get some cool air."

Fatima's cheeks were flushed, her forehead shiny and beaded with perspiration. Her handsome makeup had become splotchy and dull. The black that had outlined her eyes had become crescent smudges beneath them. "*Momken* [Maybe]," Fatima agreed.

We passed through the reception hall and greeted the elder women politely before entering a large room on the other side sparsely furnished with two thin pads on the floor. A single fluorescent bulb pretended to light the room from its perch on the wall. Pink curtains fluttered in open double windows where a group of young women hovered on the sill.

Fatima introduced me to one. Mona was curvy, dimpled and dressed in heavy makeup that had not yet smeared. Her hair was a crown of soft black ringlets. She wore a cobalt miniskirt with black fishnet stockings trimmed in crocheted roses.

"*Helwa* [Pretty]!" I complimented her stockings as we pulled a pad to sit near the window. "Did you find them in Sana'a?"

Mona stretched her legs for me to see her stockings, careful to cover her feet with her scarf to keep from offending with their bottoms. I smiled at the polite Arab protocol, which prohibits showing the bottoms of one's feet to another. Fatima whispered something to Mona. I was surprised by Fatima's stern look to her and Mona's rebellious one back. I was about to ask why when a little girl rushed into the room.

"The bride is coming! The bride is coming!" she cried.

Mona and I scrambled up from the pad, offering our hands to help Fatima. Fatima brushed away the pumpkin seeds she had been eating and hurried with us to squeeze into place in the mufraj room.

A wicker chair with a high princess back had been placed at the front of the room. It was decorated with garlands of white and blue silk flowers. Shiny white ribbons curled down the sides. I craned my neck with the other women, my eyes glued to the entrance. The women began to yell shrilly, vibrating their tongues to make their yell loud and piercing. They clapped rhythmically as the bride entered the room. Two small girls in blue satin dresses walked behind her, carrying her train.

The bride was a masterpiece. Her heavily sequined gown shimmered in the light. Her curled hair was beaded with satin roses, cascading to her puffed satin sleeves, and her makeup was flawless on her placid face. She lowered herself stiffly onto her wicker throne, her mother smoothing her train at her feet. She raised her eyes to gaze upon her audience.

Women and girls called greetings to her, filled with Mohammed's name. I did not recognize the words. "What are they saying?" I whispered to Fatima.

"They are giving blessings for a good home and many children."

Suddenly and without warning, the bride rose abruptly from her chair. The women continued to call their blessings, but the bride ignored them, dabbing her face with a damp tissue and exiting the room almost as quickly as she had entered.

I was stunned. "Is the bride supposed to leave that soon?" I whispered to Fatima. She shook her head and went to talk to Huda.

Fatima tried to keep her answer quiet when she returned. She chuckled in my ear. "The bride felt hot. She did not want her hair and makeup to be ruined by the heat."

I was astounded. "Will she come back to her guests?"

"No," Fatima said, rising from the mufraj. "Come, we can go now. The bride will not return."

We said our good-byes around the room to women who pleaded with us repeatedly and traditionally to stay. We repeated our good-byes to the older women in the reception hall. It occurred to me that they had not come into the room to welcome the bride.

When we had given adequate compliments to the bride's mother and sisters, we dug through the mounds of shoes piled by the door. We eventually found ours, and Mona handed me a package wrapped in torn newspaper. I raised my eyes in question. She smiled and walked away.

Outside, Fatima and I walked down a bumpy dirt alley to find a taxi. Unable to delay my curiosity, I opened my package under a streetlight. I stopped still in my steps.

"No!" I exclaimed. "I did not mean for Mona to give me her stockings. We must take them back."

"No, Audra," Fatima answered. "Mona has done what is right." She looked pleased.

I wanted to bite off my tongue and with it the words I had spoken to Mona. Too late I remembered that to compliment something was to obligate its owner to give it as a gift. I said nothing more as we walked toward the main street. But I felt as if I had failed.

Lord, I am not making an impact on these Muslim women. Instead they are impacting me! I cried quietly.

A taxi pulled up beside us. Fatima gave directions as I slid silently into the backseat. We rode to Fatima's house without talking, where she got out and left me with wishes for a pleasant Friday. I continued on to my house, passing burned-out streetlights and stray cats snarling with dogs over garbage. At a stoplight I watched a group of men sitting on a sidewalk, sharing stewed beans from an aluminum pan.

Lord, how many times will I fail Yemen's traditions while being caught up in my own? I asked inwardly. *How can I help them when they are giving more than I am?*

At home I showered off perfume-scented sweat and changed into an oversized T-shirt and a pair of soft leggings. I joined Kevin and the children on the mufraj and cuddled Jaden and Madison on each side with Jack on my lap in between.

I opened our worn copy of bedtime stories. "Won't we be glad when our crate comes and we have other books to read?" I asked.

Halfway through the story Jack fell asleep. The other two appeared soon to follow. I closed the book and kissed each curly head as we said our prayers together. Kevin took Jack in his arms and helped me up from the mufraj. We walked hand-in-hand to tuck Madison into her white metal cot and the boys into their brown ones.

Kevin kissed them in turn after me and went to our bedroom. I stood in the boys' doorway. Moonlight poured through their window, creating a river that flowed over their little bodies and spilled light and shadows onto the floor. A breeze ruffled the edge of their safari-print curtains. I leaned against the white plastered door frame.

As I watched them sleeping, I thought about all the Bible stories I had read and the times I had rocked them to sleep with "Jesus Loves Me." I had immersed them in the love that God poured on me.

What if they had been born Yemeni? Would I be telling them about Mohammed instead of Jesus? Was the difference only in what we had been taught?

I shook my head to clear the horrible questions that seeped in like a virus. *Lord, help me!* I cried. *Answer these doubts as only You can.*

I walked slowly to my bedroom, where Kevin was slumped against the pillows snoring softly. I caught the book that was sliding off his chest and put it on the table beside him. It was a book about Christianity and Islam.

"Lord, show me the difference," I whispered. "Then use me to show others the difference."

I kissed Kevin's cheek and turned off the light.

5

The sky rumbled with dark clouds. The scent of rain saturated the air. Kevin and I hurried the children down the sidewalks, maneuvering Jack's stroller around blowing garbage. We arrived at the *suq*, an open-air Yemeni market. On one side of the entrance women sat on the ground with round stacks of pancake-like bread. They wrapped them in newspapers and waved as we approached.

On the other side of the entrance four men displayed aluminum trolleys with mounds of glossy dates pressed together in sticky cubes. They flicked swarming flies with rags tied to sticks and called to us to sample a date.

A young man stepped out from among them, lowering a round pan of baklava and sesame-seed pastries from his shoulders. "*Hallee*, hallee [sweet]," he cried. Everyone seemed oblivious to the threat of rain.

Kevin maneuvered Jack's stroller through the suq entrance, dodging a wheelbarrow of mangoes coming out. Madison and Jaden clung to me tightly, their sides plastered against mine. We bumped into a muddy arena lined with stalls made of skinny tree trunks and thatched reed awnings. Tables under them were piled high with vegetables or fruit.

"Welcome, welcome!" vendors called, their cheeks bulging with qat.

"Let's do this quickly so we can get home before the deluge." Kevin bounced the stroller to the nearest stall.

I was glad Jack was asleep. Having had his pink cheeks pinched and his white hair stroked by the countless people we passed, he had burrowed his face deep into the corner of the stroller and fallen fast asleep.

"*Kilo tomat, loh somat, wa kilo khiyar* [A kilo of tomatoes, please, and a kilo of cucumbers]," I said, pointing.

The man grinned broadly. "Arabie good! *Tamam* [Good]!" He gave Kevin a thumbs-up sign.

Kevin practiced Arabic phrases while I shook lumps of mud off potatoes and stacked them on the vendor's scale. The fresh tomatoes and leafy greans smelled rich and earthy. My mouth watered for a bite, but I knew that camouflaged under their appearance were amoebas and other evils that could be removed only by a soak in bleach water.

The vendor waved a bunch of fresh mint at me. "*Baqshish*," he said, rewarding us for buying from him. "*Ensha'allah* [God willing] you will come back to me again."

Three young boys materialized, jostling wheelbarrows as they jockeyed for position nearest us. "*Arabeeya, arabeeya* [wheelbarrow]!" the tallest cried.

He was barefoot and not much older than Madison. His torn shirt had once been white and his muddy green pants were open at their broken fly zipper.

I smiled, thanking him, but I shook my head. "Lah, shukran. *Nemshee*. [No, thank you. We are walking.]"

When we had convinced them that our no meant no, the boys saluted and raced their wheelbarrows to compete for a woman purchasing two kilos of Lebanese squash.

Kevin and I grinned at each other. "Yemeni entrepreneurs start young," Kevin said.

"Yeah," I sighed, "but I bet they don't go to school. More illiterate adults."

We entered a concrete block building at the back of the suq. I fought the urge to hold my nose. The smell of raw fish, raw meat and animal blood surged over me. Wooden tables of melting ice were stacked with fresh seafood.

"*Gamberi,* gamberi!" A vendor waved handfuls of huge shrimp.

Another waved a squid. "*Calameri* good!"

I shook my head and walked to the meat vendors who waited across from them. They poised sharpened knives to carve meat from the piles on the tables or from the skinned animals hanging from ceiling hooks. Proudly displayed were the heads that had once been attached to the meat. Each animal had been slaughtered according to Islamic rite, bled to death by a slashed throat. Each head provided the appearance of the meat's freshness and the vendor's religious integrity.

I avoided eye contact with the men, as Fatima had taught me modest women should. I also avoided the open eyes of the animals presiding over their meat. Kevin bought two kilos of what appeared to be rump meat. I hung the bag from the stroller handle to begin our trek home. The afternoon prayer call wailed out as thunder grew louder.

"We've got to hurry, guys! Let's see how fast we can walk!" I took Madison and Jaden's hands.

"We're going to have to hustle!" Kevin pushed Jack's stroller briskly down the sidewalk.

Just as rain began to pelt us, we reached our gate out of breath. "Hurry!" I shouted. "Run for the house!"

We made it to the porch. As Kevin unlocked the door, thunder cracked and water poured from black clouds.

"That was close!" We panted in unison and ducked inside. The telephone was ringing, and I ran to answer it.

"Allo, Audra?" It was Fatima. "My *am* [uncle on father's side] died last night. The visitation for the women will be on Thursday, after tomorrow. Can you come?"

I unsnapped my balto. "I'm so sorry, Fatima. Of course I'll be there."

I hung up the phone with a sense of dread. I knew that burial took place soon after death. When a man died, Yemeni men carried the deceased's body on an open cot with a beating drum and a procession of male friends who called out words about Mohammed on their way to the cemetery. Afterward the deceased was honored with long hours of loudspeaker Quran recitations that wailed like monotonous pain. I did not know what to expect from the women.

On Thursday I scoured my wardrobe for a black outfit to wear to the funeral visitation. I had purchased tea, sugar and tinned milk, as instructed by Fatima. A woman's hospitality requirements were not relieved during difficult times. Since many women would gather, friends were expected to help supply refreshments. I heard the telephone ring as I pulled a black blouse from my wardrobe. I turned to see Kevin standing in the doorway. His face was somber, his eyes looking cautiously at mine.

"What's up?" I asked.

"Nigel called." He paused and took a deep breath. "Sweetheart, they've lost our crates. The Boones' crate arrived in port on schedule, and ours were supposed to be with theirs, but they weren't. The freight company can't track them. They seem to have disappeared."

My legs gave way, and I sat down on my shirt on the bed. I stared at him as words began to stumble out. "They've . . . they've lost them?" I shook my head in disbelief. "Will they be able to find them?"

Kevin shrugged. "Nobody knows. They traced them to Jordan, but there's no trace after that."

Tears stung my eyes. "Do they think they were stolen?"

"They don't know. Maybe." Kevin sat down, putting his arm around my shoulders. "They'll keep trying to find them. If they don't, insurance will replace everything."

I shook his arm from my shoulders. "No, it won't!" I cried. "I don't want it replaced. I want the things we had! Our things!"

Kevin fidgeted with his hands. "I know, honey." He raised one hand slowly to smooth my hair. "We'll just have to do the best we can."

I sat on the bed, feeling as dark as the black clothing I would wear. I dressed and kissed the children good-bye, leaving them with cheerful words I did not feel.

The widow lived in an unpainted concrete block house with a flat tin roof and an unfinished room on the side. A pen of sheep bleated at the back of the dirt yard where children ran barefoot in the dust. Sofia, Fatima's cousin and sister-in-law, greeted me at the door. She was my height with light skin and hair dyed to a reddish blond. She was dressed in a tight black jumper with a black turtleneck underneath.

Sofia solemnly kissed both of my cheeks. "Shukran [thank you]," she said softly, taking the tea, sugar and milk. She led me toward the mufraj room.

I caught a glimpse of Fatima as we passed the kitchen. Dressed in a thin housedress, Fatima was bent over a plastic tub filled with soapy water. Dirty cooking pots were stacked around her on the concrete floor. I started to object, knowing Fatima suffered back pain as she approached her eighth month of pregnancy. But Sofia hurried me past. I reluctantly complied. I knew my interference would embarrass Fatima, who would not want to be seen in that position.

But I would not let it go. I pretended I had not seen her. "Where is Fatima?" I asked Sofia. "I must see her."

I hoped to rescue her from her chores as a new wife in her mother-in-law's house.

"She is coming. Sit, sit." Sofia gestured toward the thick red and black mufraj cushions.

I sat. I was apparently early; no one else had arrived. I had not yet learned that times given for arrival were earlier than times intended.

"I am coming after five minutes," Sofia said, trying to look apologetic about leaving me. I nodded.

I took off my balto cloak in the quiet room and let my black hejab [head scarf] slip from my hair to my shoulders. I unlatched the window and pushed the dark drapes aside to invite fresh air into the somber room. I tried to see the sky, but my view was marred by a wall. I could see only a sliver of blue.

I sighed, wishing I could be up in the sky. I wanted to see the earth as a map spread with boundaries and destinations. *Then I could find our crates,* I thought to myself.

I looked at the sliver of sky. "You have the right perspective, don't You, Lord?" I whispered. "We see mazes and lose sight of our destination. But You see it all, all the time." I closed my eyes. "You see the end from the beginning. You are never confused by what is in between." I thought of the doubts that reared periodically to torment me. "You are never confused, Lord. Help me not to be."

I slumped down on the mufraj with a heavy sigh and traced the paisley rug with my black stockinged toe. It was pretty, a flourish of mauves and reds and black. I picked up an edge of the huge rug. Hiding underneath was ugly gray concrete. I dropped the rug quickly and tucked my feet under my skirt as Sofia entered the room with her widowed mother.

I rose to kiss the elderly woman and murmur sympathetic words. Around fifty years old, she was heavyset with gray-streaked hair and a caramel complexion surrounding sharp, dark eyes. She walked slowly to the center of the mufraj and took her place.

Two women trailed in behind her, each walking over to kiss her and murmur a medley of phrases I had not heard before. The widow responded with a series of words I did not understand. Other women entered, removing their veils and loosening their hejabs as they formed a solemn line to greet the widow. They repeated the same phrases injected with Mohammed's name. Tears began to stream down the widow's cheeks as she accepted kisses from each visitor and replied to their sympathies.

One woman was covered in more black than the others. She brusquely removed her black gloves and lifted her veil. Her jaw seemed to jut out at the sides, and her dark eyes were narrow. To my horror, the woman began to scold the widow loudly. I understood her Arabic.

"You must not cry. It is *harram* [forbidden]," the woman admonished. "You must say *al hamdulilah* [praise the God]. Your husband's death was the will of the God. It was his fate. It is for you to say al hamdulilah without complaint or tears." The woman dabbed the widow's face brusquely with a clean, pink tissue.

"Yes, yes." The other women nodded. "Al hamdulilah. It was the will of God."

Looking ashamed and humiliated, the widow bowed her head. She wiped her eyes with another proffered tissue. "Al hamdulilah," she whispered slowly. "Al hamdulilah."

The black-shrouded woman ceased her scolding and seated herself opposite the widow. She folded her arms and nodded a thin smile at the approving faces around her.

It made me angry. I wanted to jump from my seat and shout, "No! That is not what God is like!"

I wanted to tell them about how Jesus had enveloped me with His love when my husband had been dying. I wanted them to know the living hope of One who spared people from eternal death. But I said nothing. I looked around at the women, their faces satisfied with the moment, and I kept silent, imprisoned by my own intimidation.

The widow straightened herself against her cushions and sat almost regally with her hands folded in her lap. She retrieved her black hejab and draped it around her hair again, fixing her empty, dark eyes on an obscure corner of the floor and keeping them there. She seemed to have covered not only her hair but also her heart.

Another woman entered the room. She was around sixty and was dressed in black taffeta. Her heavy walk was punctuated by a limp. Two women moved to make room for her beside the widow. She sat down and adjusted her wide skirts, crossing her thick ankles underneath them. Rather than greet the women individually, she kissed the insides of her chubby hands, then opened them outward, greeting the women inclusively as a group. The women murmured their responses in unison.

The newcomer appeared to be a holy woman in charge of the visitation. She wiped her hands on her black scarf, opened a carved wooden stand and placed a gold-leaf Quran on it. She cleared her throat.

Just before she began her recitation, Fatima entered, her head low as she scurried across the room apologetically. She slid in next to me on the mufraj and whispered quick greetings to me and the women around her. She was breathing hard, her face wet and her arms damp where she had just washed them. She adjusted her black crepe dress as Sofia shot a disapproving scowl. I squeezed Fatima's hand, smiling back at her grateful response.

The holy woman began to chant the Quran like a song without a melody. I noticed that she did not look at the Quran in front of her but recited memorized words. I wondered if she could read; most Yemeni women could not.

At several pauses in the recitation, three women injected phrases about Mohammed that elicited responses chanted in unison by the others. I wondered if the women understood the meaning of what they were reciting. I had once asked Fatima about the meaning of a Quranic passage. She had not been able to explain it; she did not understand it herself. But she emphasized the beauty of how it was phrased and the language that had been used to say it. What it meant had been insignificant.

The woman continued her recitation, pausing in rhythmic breaks to inject Mohammed's name. A fervor seemed to be growing. The tempo was changing. The holy woman's chant became faster and increased in pitch. The women's responses grew louder, more intense. Each face was locked on the holy woman. Even the widow seemed oblivious to her pain as she responded with the others.

The room felt oppressive. I found myself taking deeper breaths, as if the room did not have enough air. I looked at the window I had secretly opened, wishing I had opened it wider. The recitation continued to grow faster and louder until it reached a peak. Then suddenly everything stopped, ebbing down like an engine slowing to a halt. The women became silent.

The holy woman lifted the Quran, kissed it and passed it worshipfully to the woman seated next to her, who held it reverently and also kissed it before passing it to the woman beside her. The process continued around the room until each woman except me had kissed the Quran. It had been carefully handed around me. Considered to be an infidel, I was not allowed to touch it with my unclean hands.

After the Quran was settled gently back onto its wooden stand, Fatima rose from the mufraj. "I'll be back," she whispered, hurrying away.

I looked over at the widow. When she had chanted her responses to the Quran, her eyes had sparkled with dark intensity and she had seemed exhilarated. But now the rose in her cheeks and the shine in her eyes were fading. As she sank back against her cushions, she seemed to be sinking back into her empty place.

Fatima returned carrying a tray loaded with hot, sweet tea. She served the oldest women first, beginning with the widow. Even though I was an infidel Christian, I was served with them because of my status as a foreign guest. Fatima served each woman, hurrying back to the kitchen in between servings to rinse the limited number of teacups. Then she motioned for me to join her at the door. It was almost *maghreb*, the evening prayer call.

"I want to go home. I am tired. I have been here from the morning." Fatima leaned heavily on my arm as we walked toward the main street to flag a taxi.

"You were busy today," I ventured.

"Yes, my aunt gave me much work." She sighed deeply. "She has two daughters, but she gave the work to me, big like this." She patted her bulging middle. "She makes me khidamah [servant] in her house." She blinked away the tears before they could fall. "I don't know why she treats me so badly."

"Does her son treat you badly, too?" I asked cautiously.

"No, he is a good husband. I obey him, and he treats me well. But what can he do? If he speaks to his mother, she treats me worse. She is his mother; what can he say?" She clenched her jaw. "She has a black heart. Her son loves me, and now she hates me."

"Maybe she is jealous, Fatima. You told me a mother raises her son to love her so that he will take care of her if her husband dies or takes another wife. Maybe your mother-in-law doesn't want her son loving any woman but her."

Fatima sighed. "Yes, that is true. It happened to my friends. But I did not think it would happen to me."

I linked my arm through Fatima's. "Maybe when the baby is born your mother-in-law will change. Maybe she will . . . Owww!" My yelp stopped me from finishing my sentence. The sting of a sharp rock hit my back between my shoulders. Another rock skipped on the dirt, sailing inches from Fatima. I turned. Three boys were snickering in the shadows of a garbage Dumpster.

"*Lah* [No]!" I shouted. "Harram [Forbidden]!"

Fatima stopped me, clicking her tongue. "No, no, Audra. You must not. They are children!" She squelched the scolding I was about to lash out. "They are little boys, not ten years old. You must not scold them."

I was stunned. "Fatima! They could have hit you or your baby!" I stopped short of scolding her. "They cannot do this—it is wrong! They are old enough to learn that this is wrong."

Fatima laughed at me. "Come, Audra. They are only playing. They are boys! Leave them. Look, here is a taxi."

I was stinging from the pain in my shoulder but more from the snickering behind the Dumpster. I wanted to correct their wrong. But I relented when Fatima asked me again. I quietly climbed into the taxi behind her.

We approached the road to my house, and I leaned forward to stop the driver. Fatima grabbed my arm, a look of panic flooding her face. "Audra, please. Go with me to my house first," she whispered in English.

"Why?" I frowned. I was eager to get home, and we were only a block from my house. "My family is waiting for me. I need to fix their supper."

"Please, Audra," she pleaded, dropping her voice lower. "I don't want to ride in the taxi alone." She laughed uncertainly. "I am afraid."

"Afraid? But then I will be alone to ride back to my house!" I exclaimed, bewildered.

"Please, Audra," she repeated. "You are different. You are *qawia* [strong]. You are not afraid." She laughed nervously again. "I am afraid of the driver. He will not hurt you. He will bring you back to your house quickly."

I did not want to do it. I was tired and eager to rid myself of my heavy trappings. But I was touched by her fear, even as it surprised me. I nodded reluctantly and sat back in the seat, listening to her sigh of relief as she relaxed beside me. I watched my street sail past.

After telling Fatima good-bye, I sat quietly as the taxi turned and headed back in the direction we had come. I looked up at the stars that were beginning to twinkle in the darkening sky. *Lord, I don't understand these women,* I prayed silently. *They are bolder than I am to speak up for their religion, but they are afraid of being alone in a taxi. Help me understand this, Lord. Help me be as unapologetic about my faith as they are about theirs.*

I paid the driver and opened the gate to my home.

Twelve hours later I leaned back on our mufraj cushions and searched the window for the sunrise. I watched as dawn kept its gray wrapped around the sun. It seemed to tease me, letting bits of light peek like yellow petals from a closed bud. Slowly the dawn peeled back and the sun burst into flower. The sky blossomed with gold and pink.

I sipped my tea, watching the light fan out and purge the darkness. I stared at the pages of my opened Bible. My soul felt parched and thirsty. I longed to drink deep from God's Word, but questions haunted me.

Lord, if I had been raised to believe Islam, would I believe Mohammed to be God's messenger as strongly as I believe Jesus is the Messiah? The question was like a worm eating at my faith.

I leaned back in my chair, remembering Fatima's prayers as she knelt on her prayer rug. I thought of God's name invoked on the street and in every part of Yemeni life.

Missionaries are not supposed to have doubts, Lord. But these questions worm into my head, and I cannot seem to keep them out. Help me to see beyond them to You. I left my chair to prepare for the day.

At lunchtime a gusty wind blew grit against our closed glass windows as our midday meal of grilled chicken, rice and *mushakel* [mixed vegetables] steamed on our dining room table. Kevin had brought the meal home from a *mata'am* [restaurant], a small room crowded with boisterous men and flaming butane cookers that, like many street-side cafes, did not offer a family room where women could eat. Jaden and Jack waited for me to carve their chicken legs. Madison picked cardamom pods out of her rice as Kevin tore a piece of *khobz* [flatbread] to scoop his.

"Well, summer is almost over," I said, licking my fingers. "Jaden, you'll get to ride the bus with Madison to school. First grade!"

Before anyone could answer, a huge cracking sound ripped through our conversation, ending our words with a loud thud. We all stared at each other, then raced in unison to the window. We strained to peer outside, but we could see only a little of the yard.

A head taller than I, Kevin pressed against the glass. "It looks like a tree fell over," he said.

"A tree?" I shrieked. "Our tree? The tree the kids are always climbing?" All five of us ran into the yard.

The short, wiry tree that had held the children in its skinny arms was lying on its side, completely uprooted. Its gnarled roots were exposed, naked for all to see. We stood staring at it. My first instinct was to pat dirt back around the roots. I wanted to cover them, to restore the tree to its former glory. It hurt to see it in such a position after the children had played in its branches. I shivered. I was glad the children had not been caught in its fall.

I peered inside the trunk, studying the scrawny tangle of roots. "Hey, Kevin, look at this. It's hollow. This tree has been dead for a long time."

Kevin bent over to look. "You're right. All this time we thought it was alive and well, but it was only a matter of time."

The children picked at the crackling leaves. I had not noticed before that the leaves were brown.

"Can we still climb on it, Daddy?" Jaden asked.

"No, honey," Kevin answered. "It is too dangerous with the insides dried out."

"Why did it fall down?" Madison asked.

"Its roots weren't getting any water or food from the soil," I explained. "It did not have anything underneath to hold on to. That old wind just knocked it right over."

"Oh." Madison peeked cautiously inside the trunk. "It was a good tree."

I nodded. "It looked like it, didn't it? Now it's just firewood. We'll have to chop it up and burn it. Maybe we can roast marshmallows."

"Yummy." Jack's face lit up.

"Well, come on, guys. Let's go finish our lunch." I waved the children to join me.

I looked back again at the lifeless tree. It had appeared so strong. I shuddered. I did not want to think what its deception could have cost my children.

6

School was a week away. With the children's school clothing lost in our crates, I busied myself making new ones. I was sewing black Scotty dogs on a red gingham blouse for Madison when the telephone rang. I answered it.

"Asalam alaykum [Peace be upon you]." It was Mona, Fatima's friend. She gushed the news that Fatima had given birth early that morning to a baby boy. Mona, Sofia and Fatima's mother-in-law had been with her for the delivery.

I tried to ignore my hurt feelings at not being included. I knew I was still a foreigner in Fatima's eyes. I listened to Mona chat lightly about Fatima and the baby. I drummed my fingers on the table, putting little effort into following her fast-spoken words. Something in her manner irritated me. It seemed false and contrived. She skirted over a brief mention of the baby's illness.

I stopped drumming my fingers and interrupted her midsentence. "*Marah thanya, loh samaty* [Another time, please]. How is the baby sick? What is wrong?"

Mona brushed aside my questions, whispering, "Ma'a sha'allah [What God wills]." I knew the phrase was commonly spoken around infants and children like a charm to ward off evil. I had been warned to say ma'a sha'allah over my own children. I had responded, "I walk with God through Jesus. Jesus is all I need."

Mona was not giving me a straight answer about the baby, and I knew something was wrong. "May I visit Fatima at the hospital?" I asked.

"Yes, yes, you must," Mona replied. "She is asking for you."

I hung up the phone and telephoned Alison, a physician friend from Europe. Deaths among Yemeni children were not uncommon. Most of the women I knew had lost at least one child under the age of five, and I wanted to prevent Fatima's baby from becoming a statistic among them. I explained my concern to Alison. "Will you go with me to see Fatima?" She agreed.

Alison and I arrived at the hospital late that afternoon. We found Fatima's private room, but she was not in it. The white-robed, white-veiled nurse told us she was with her baby, who had been taken for tests. She said they would return "after one hour." Knowing this probably meant three or four hours, we decided to leave. I jotted a note in English and laid it on the white-sheeted cot next to an empty steel crib.

Alison flipped through a clipboard tied to the crib. The report had been written in English, as most medical documents were, and detailed the infant's birth. Alison clicked her tongue. The baby had been born with the umbilical cord wrapped around his neck. Attempts to resuscitate him were successful after an hour of effort by the physician.

Alison let the clipboard fall back with a bang against the crib. "If the baby lives, he will have severe brain damage," she said grimly. "According to this report, he is unable to swallow, and he is choking on his own saliva."

A group of four women walked into the room, including Fatima's mother-in-law and Huda, the bride's mother from the wedding I had attended. I did not know the other two. They hugged us enthusiastically, exclaiming over the birth of Fatima's son. Even Fatima's mother-in-law seemed proud that Fatima had delivered a boy.

I nodded my head, forcing a smile. I wondered if they understood what had happened, or if they were ignoring the truth. *Will they soon be telling Fatima to accept her fate and say* al hamdulilah? I wondered.

The mother-in-law seemed to guess my thoughts. She looked forcefully at me. "Ensha'allah, he will be strong, qawi, like his father. Ma'a sha'allah [What God wills]."

The other women agreed in unison, "Ma'a sha'allah, ma'a sha'allah."

I whispered, "Ensha'allah [God willing]." Alison said nothing.

We quietly took our leave as the women sat down to chat on Fatima's bed. We glanced at the empty crib, declining protests to stay and celebrate.

Two days later Kevin and I loaded the children into an agency van to drive to the home of Shirley and Johnny Higdon, colleagues with children near the ages of ours. They lived near the public hospital where Fatima's baby had been transferred. We pulled out of our graveled yard and into the street. When Kevin got out of the car to close our wide iron gates, I heard a child screaming. I craned my neck to locate the screams but could not see anything.

"It's the neighbor's little girl," Madison said, pointing outside her window.

"Yeah, her brothers are hurting her," added Jaden.

I looked where they were pointing. In front of their father's *baqala* [grocery store], a laughing boy of about ten gripped both arms of his screaming sister, who was around five. I gasped as their teenaged brother swung the youngest boy, a toddler, hard and fast at his captive sister so that his feet kicked her full force in her upper thighs. The boys laughed outright as the little girl screamed and writhed from each blow. The wailing child wriggled and pulled, ripping her rose-colored dress in an attempt to escape their iron grasp.

I hammered the window with my fist as I rolled it down. "Lah [No]!" I shouted at them. "Harram! *Hatha mosh tamam!* [Forbidden! This is not good!]" The boys sneered scornfully at me and continued to torment their sister.

"Kevin!" I yelled through the window, pointing at the boys. "Do something! They won't listen to me."

When Kevin saw where I was pointing, he strode his six-foot, two-hundred-pound bulk angrily toward the boys. He was twice the size of the average Yemeni man. When the boys saw him coming, they stopped their laughing and re-linquished their hold on the sobbing little girl, who quickly darted for their backyard.

Sputtering with anger, Kevin scolded the boys as well as he could in Arabic. The boys only shrugged, snickering and nudging each other, impatient for Kevin to finish. When he had, they hurried into the backyard after their sister.

Kevin was furious. He stalked up the stairs to the baqala and stuck his head through the door. But he did not go in. Instead he turned abruptly and stalked back down the stairs toward the car. He was shaking, his teeth clenched tight.

"What happened?" I asked as he got into the car. He ground the gear into first, ripping the cuff of his sleeve on the gearshift.

"Their father and two other men were chewing qat right by the window." He spat out the words with disgust. "They saw the whole thing. They just did not care."

My head hit the headrest as Kevin jerked the car into the street. I strained my neck to see the neighbor's backyard as we passed. I could not see if the boys had recaptured their sister.

"Thank the Lord Fatima's baby is a boy," I whispered. Kevin nodded his silent agreement.

We deposited our children in the Higdons' courtyard. Leaving the fathers to talk projects over coffee and contemporary Christian music, Shirley and I made our way to the public hospital.

Inside a narrow door, infants and mothers roomed together in a long ward crowded with iron cots and small wooden incubators. Shirley and I wove our way between them, murmuring polite greetings to each new mother and grandmother we passed. Each wore a balto and tried to keep her hejab wrapped as she leaned against the iron rails of her headboard or sat swinging her feet off the side of her bed.

The women gestured as we passed, wanting us to see the babies bound in blanket cocoons inside the glass boxes. One infant had a cleft palate. Another had a malformed hand. The mothers patted spaces on their beds for us to sit, moving aside plastic bags of clothing. There were no televisions, only a large, black-rimmed clock that ticked hours on a peeling, white wall.

One woman held out a section of the orange she was eating. "*Ahlen wa sahlen* [Hello and welcome]," she said eagerly. I smiled at her club-footed infant and hesitated, about to take the orange. Fatima called from the end of the ward. She waved impatiently for us.

"Shukran [Thank you]," I murmured apologetically and moved on.

When we reached Fatima, she hugged me tightly, kissing both sides of my face three times before letting me go. She kept hold of my hand even as she hugged Shirley. She moved aside her plastic bags and motioned for us to sit on her cot.

"I am glad to see you!" she cried.

"I am glad to see you, too! How are you?" I asked, still holding her hand.

Shirley adjusted the blond hair that had strayed from her scarf in the force of Fatima's hug. Her light freckled skin looked flushed and her blue eyes were misty at the warmth of Fatima's welcome.

Fatima wrinkled her nose in a grimace. "I am good. There is some pain still. But I am okay."

She pulled me to the incubator at her bedside. "See my son." Her smile was proud and tender. "His name is Qasar. It means 'emperor.' "

Shirley and I moved closer to the tiny baby, who was wrapped tightly in white sheeting, lying inside the framed glass box like a miniature mummy with only his curly head exposed. An oxygen tube was taped into his tiny nose. His breathing was irregular, and he coughed frequently, choking and struggling with each cough and making an effort to cry.

Fatima cringed at each sound. "My baby cannot swallow or suck his milk," she told Shirley. "The doctor said ensha'allah [God willing] he will be better and he will grow to be strong and healthy."

She looked at the infant and then back at Shirley. "But he cannot swallow."

Fatima scoured Shirley's somber face. Shirley was an American nurse and was respected as much as a doctor by local women. "Do you think he will become well soon?" she asked softly.

I ached at the worry in Fatima's weary eyes. Her face looked gaunt and hungry for hope. I squeezed her hand tightly as we stood together by the incubator. I wanted to infuse her with hope. But I wanted it to be real hope rooted in living Truth, so that it could not be taken away.

Shirley cleared her throat. I had seen her flash of anger when Fatima described the doctor's prognosis. Shirley had little tolerance for the local practice of telling patients what they wanted to hear instead of the truth. She had been by the bedside of dying patients who had clung to such lies. They had been kept from the truth until their diseased bodies were beyond restoration. And then it had been too late.

"Fatima," Shirley began gently, taking Fatima's other hand in hers. "If the baby cannot swallow, he cannot drink or eat. He must learn to swallow or he cannot survive."

Fatima nodded, tears filling her eyes, as she looked at Shirley and then me. The anguish in her eyes hurt my soul. Shirley dropped Fatima's hand and reached inside the incubator to stroke the infant's tiny head.

"Fatima," I hesitated. "May we pray for your baby?" I held my breath for her rejection.

"Yes, yes, please," Fatima answered instantly. She did not notice the women who might be watching. She did not seem to care. She eagerly pulled us closer to her baby.

I was stunned by her response. Fatima had never allowed me to mention Jesus' name. But now she seemed hungry for it. We hovered over the incubator. I placed my hand on the baby's back as Shirley placed hers on his head. We bowed our heads slightly and prayed discreetly with open eyes.

Shirley prayed first, then I. We laid the infant before God, asking God in Jesus' name to help the baby swallow so that he could eat and be nourished. We finished and stood silently beside Fatima.

Fatima's eyes were glistening with tears. "Thank you," she whispered. "Thank you." She looked wistfully through the glass box at her tiny son.

A light dawned in Shirley. "Fatima," she asked. "Have you held your baby?"

Fatima shook her head, shaking away a tear. "Not since he was in the private hospital. Here the nurse said I cannot. She said Qasar must stay in the incubator, even for the tube feedings."

Anger flashed again in Shirley's eyes. The baby was not attached to IV lines or to any machine other than the oxygen tank. There was nothing to obstruct his being held by his mother. Shirley raised the wooden lid of the incubator and gently lifted the infant out.

"Of course you can hold your baby," she said. "He needs your touch, and you need his."

Fatima took the infant carefully into her arms, holding him near her breast. She gently lowered her cheek to caress his head against it. She closed her eyes, savoring the feel of her son. Tears streamed down her bowed face.

"Fatima," Shirley said. "You can hold your baby whenever you want. It is good for him to feel your touch. When you lift him out of the incubator, keep the tube from slipping by holding him like this." She demonstrated. "And tell the nurse I said you could," she added gruffly.

Gratitude flowed wordlessly from Fatima's wet eyes. She sat between us on the bed with her son in her arms. For a while she said nothing. She rocked him gently, taking him to a quiet place in her thoughts. Her grip on him slowly relaxed.

Fatima began to chat, introducing other women nearby and pointing out their babies as the mothers smiled proudly. One woman held out bananas. Another held up the prayer cap she was crocheting.

"Tamam [Good]," I said.

Fatima chatted pleasantly through the hour, never once releasing her hold on her son. Then Shirley began gathering her hejab and handbag to leave.

Fatima reached out to clasp my arm, gripping me to the bed. "No, please, Audra. Stay with me. Only one hour more."

I looked at Shirley. I knew that Kevin and the children would be waiting to go home. It was near suppertime. But I could not walk away from Fatima's pleading eyes.

"You could stay a little longer," Shirley suggested, wrapping her hejab. "I can give the kids a snack, and Kevin can pick you up later."

I hesitated. Fatima tightened her grip on my arm. "Please," she whispered, "only a little longer."

I nodded to Shirley. "Thanks," I said. "Tell Kevin I'll be by the front gate at five o'clock."

After Shirley left, Fatima smiled wide at me. She turned the baby to display him again. "He is going to be strong," she said proudly. "I have a son!"

"*Mahbrook* [Congratulations]! I came to see him after he was born, but you were not in your room. Did the women tell you?" I asked.

Her face darkened. "Yes," she said tersely. "They told me."

I searched her eyes. "What's wrong, Fatima? Did something happen?"

"No, nothing." She hesitated. "My friends came to see me at the private hospital only. When we moved to the public hospital, no one came."

"No one? None of your friends has been to see you for two days?" I was shocked.

"You only," she answered. "My mother-in-law will come after tomorrow. And my husband comes to bring food, but he cannot stay with the women."

She took my hand and squeezed it, holding it close. "You are my friend," she whispered.

The next afternoon as I walked into the ward Fatima bolted from her reclining position and stood tapping her feet until I reached her. Her eyes were shining like polished stones. Grinning broadly, she hugged me, hurrying through the formal greetings.

"Audra!" she said breathlessly. "Qasar is much better today! The doctor says he can swallow. He will soon take his milk from a bottle, not the tube!"

"Al hamdulilah," I replied. "God has done this, Fatima. We asked Him in Jesus' name."

"*Akeed* [Of course]." Fatima lifted the baby from the incubator, careful not to dislodge his oxygen tube. "Ensha'allah, he will grow strong! Ensha'allah."

"Ensha'allah," I whispered.

Fatima laid the sleeping infant back in his incubator. We sat on the bed to begin our chat but were interrupted by someone calling from across the room.

"Fatima!" It was Huda, the bride's mother from the wedding. Two of her daughters hovered behind her, peeking out to look warily at us. They waved, delighted that we had seen them. They huddled close and bumped between the crowded cots, their eyes wide with fright as their glances darted between Fatima and the other women in the ward. They would not look at the incubators or the babies in them.

When they reached us, they hugged Fatima quickly and rushed breathlessly through their greetings. Still pressed tightly together, they cooed hurriedly over Qasar, reaching into the incubator to pinch his cheek.

"Ma'a sha'allah, ma'a sha'allah" they repeated.

I looked around the room, bewildered by their odd behavior. I tried to see what was frightening them. I could see only babies and their mothers and the single, white-veiled nurse who moved between them.

Fatima made room for them and patted her cot, but they would not sit down. They continued to clutch each other, averting their eyes from everything except us. Then, as quickly as they had entered, they abruptly whispered their good-byes and left. Still clinging tightly together, they bumped back through the cots and scurried out of the ward.

I turned my gaping mouth to Fatima. "What was that all about?" I asked. "What was wrong?"

Fatima waved her hand in the air, unbothered by their behavior or my astonishment. "They do not like hospitals," she said casually. "They are afraid from them."

I was confused. "Afraid of what?" I looked back toward the entrance.

Fatima smiled and took my hand. "You are qawia, Audra, strong in your heart. You do not understand this."

She tucked my hand into hers. "When the doctor tells me to take Qasar home, we will plan my forty-day party. It is a big celebration, like a wedding. You must be there with me."

I nodded, still staring at the entrance. I could not comprehend the fear that Fatima obviously accepted. "Fatima, what are they afraid of?" I repeated.

Fatima sighed. "Life. Death. *Khalas* [Enough], Audra. Khalas. You do not understand this. Will you come to my forty-day party? You must be with me."

I looked back at Fatima and blinked. "Akeed [Of course]! I would love to." I looked at the sleeping infant. "I will continue to pray for Qasar. I will ask my friends to pray, too."

"Yes, yes, you must," Fatima whispered. "You must."

We celebrated Qasar's birth with a beautiful party at Fatima's apartment 44 days after his birth. Fatima was right; it was like a wedding, complete with lovely dresses and overdone makeup. I shared Fatima's joy, humbled when she gave me the place of honor next to her. We sat together at the front of the room. Women called out blessings in Mohammed's name as I cringed. I thanked the Lord for sparing Qasar's life.

The first week of September passed, and Madison and Jaden began school. I stood by the gate as they climbed onto the bus together. I waved as they pulled away, my heart catching in my throat. "First day of school," I sighed.

That afternoon Kevin came racing into our bedroom. "Guess what!" he hollered, bouncing onto the bed.

I looked up from the blouse I was ironing. "What?"

"I just got off the phone with Nigel. They found our crates! They were in Jordan! They were taken off the ship by mistake. They have been sitting on the dock this whole time!"

I leaped toward Kevin, catching the tottering iron before it fell to the floor. "I can't believe it! I can't believe it!" I shouted.

"Me neither! They are supposed to arrive in Hudaydah tomorrow and be trucked to Sana'a next week!"

Madison, Jaden and Jack hurried into our room with panicked eyes. I grabbed their hands. "They found our crates! Our stuff from home!" I cried.

"Our books and toys?" Madison asked.

"Yes, honey! Everything! They'll bring them to us next week!" I danced with them around the room. "They found them!" I cried. "They found them!"

Eight days later our crates were delivered to our house. Trucked all night from Hudaydah, they arrived at our gate at 5:30 in the morning. I watched from the window as Kevin directed the semitrailer to back through our gate. Neighborhood men returning from prayers clustered to watch the truck park in our driveway.

Two men jumped out of the cab and climbed on top of the crates. They pried them open to hoist boxes onto the backs of waiting men and braced them until the men steadied themselves under the weight. I was amazed by their strength. They were short, wiry men barely taller than I and not much heavier, yet they carried boxes double their weight, groaning and grunting as they stacked them on our front porch.

I cringed as a huge box tottered back and forth. Shouts in Arabic thundered when the box fell with a thud to the ground. I turned away from the window.

I coaxed the children into eating most of their breakfast before their school bus arrived. Shirley took Jack to her house to play. I tucked my hair into my hejab and rolled up my sleeves.

Kevin hauled boxes into the living room, and I sorted their contents, creating mounds on the floor that quickly evolved into chaos. Because we had been allowed to pack according to volume not weight, we had filled every possible crack with items such as toothpaste, underwear, socks and sewing thread. I sorted clothes and carried cooking pans into the kitchen, singing praises to God that our crates had been delivered.

"You are Lord over everything," I whispered. "You are Messiah! The living Lord!" I carried another armload into the bathroom.

I felt God nudge my heart. I stopped walking. I wanted to shelve the nudge to ponder in a quieter moment when I was not so busy. But I knew God was speaking to me.

I laid an armful of towels on the floor and went to my bedroom to sit on the bed. *Okay, Lord. Here I am. What are You trying to tell me?*

The words of praise I had just said came back to me: "You are Messiah. The living Lord."

Suddenly other words returned to me, words I had prayed weeks before but had locked away when our crates had been lost: *Lord, could You bring in our crates the week after school starts?*

My heart began pounding. I focused on the voice of God moving in me.

I remembered more questions I had asked the Lord: *If I had been raised to believe Islam, would I be a devout*

Muslim instead of a devout Christian? Was the difference only in what we had been taught?

In the quiet of my beating heart, the answer whispered clearly: *You asked for your crates to arrive the week after the children began school. The Boones' crates were delivered on time, but your crates were lost, beyond the reach of man. Yet I knew where they were and when they would be delivered. Now you have your crates, delivered at the time you asked. Only I could do that.*

Tears began to fill my eyes. I sat quietly, understanding the answer I had been seeking, an answer that had been with me all along. The difference in my faith was that Jesus is alive. I talked with Him, and He talked with me because He was not someone dead and gone. He interactively and authoritatively reigned in my life. Whether I had been taught about Him or taught about someone else did not change who He is. It did not stop His living presence. No teaching or religion could change or substitute that.

I remembered Fatima's words. *"You are qawia, strong in your heart."* I realized that what made me strong was living strength, given by Someone who could only supply it if He was alive.

"You are Messiah!" I whispered.

I wiped my face and stood by the window, gazing into the cloudless, blue sky. I looked at the yard and saw the ruts in the gravel where the truck had been. Next to them was a mound of dirt that looked like a grave in a cemetery. It was the hole we had filled that had been left by the uprooted tree, a tree that had appeared strong on the outside but had been dead on the inside. It had no living source to nourish and sustain it. It became firewood.

I looked again at the sky. "Thank You, Lord," I whispered. "Thank You for answering my doubts and helping me remember the difference."

I returned to my unpacking. My excitement over our belongings had waned. I was in awe of God, humbled by His attentiveness to me. Jesus had again proven enough to meet my need, and I was content to trust Him.

But I would not remain content. Little did I know that in the months ahead a greater question of trust loomed. Only then, God would ask the question of me.

7

The mountains seemed dipped in the pale blue ink of the October sky. But they were darker, like smudges in watercolor. They floated far beyond the concrete buildings jutting out above me like rocks from an ocean. Looking up at the blue, I walked crooked on the sidewalk, practicing my Arabic but thinking of endless sky.

I recited words from my lesson, rolling them around on my tongue, interchanging verb forms. I passed a man sitting in a doorway with mounds of raw cotton spilling out around him. He was stuffing the inside of a mufraj cushion, packing it with the hilt of his curved *jambiya* [dagger].

"Where you from?" The man's r's were heavily rolled.

I flipped mentally through my vocabulary, searching for the words he had spoken. I had not heard them before and could not place their meaning. I was two blocks away before I realized the words he had spoken were English.

I kept walking. I entered the street next to mine and was startled by a loud noise coming from two streets away. People were shouting amid the sound of breaking glass, metal clangs and thuds. I slowed my walk to peer down the alley.

A man ran up from the side street. He screamed at me, waving his arms frantically with a volley of Arabic too rushed for me to understand. He ducked into a doorway, turning once more to rant before slamming his door behind him. I kept walking, craning periodically to look back at the bolted doorway.

Another man appeared from the alley, with another close on his heels. Both were running. They had tucked their long *thob* tunics into their knee-length boxer shorts so their legs would be free to run even faster. They, too, screamed at me and waved wildly with their arms. I caught the word *besurah* [quickly], and I accelerated my pace until I was running. I did not look back again. I reached my gate out of breath and thrust my key into the lock.

The gate would not open. It had been bolted with the bar from the inside. The shouting and banging grew louder behind me. I hammered on our iron gate.

"Kevin! It's me!" I shouted. "I can't get in!" I pounded harder. The noise was getting closer. "Kevin!" I screamed.

The gate cracked open less than a foot and an arm grabbed mine, yanking me inside. It was Nicolaus, the colleague in charge of our team's security.

"Praise God you're safe!" he said. "Are you okay?" He bolted the iron bar behind me.

"What on earth is going on? I'm fine. What's this all about?" I smoothed my sleeve down and rubbed my arm.

"There's a riot in Tahrir Square, and it's moving this way. They're smashing windows, denting cars, breaking anything they can find. They would love to get hold of a foreigner right now."

I felt my eyes grow wide. "That's what those men were telling me. But why? What for?"

"The price of gasoline and flour went up—almost doubled. The people are rioting against the government for the price increases."

Panic began to choke my voice. "Kevin's not back?" I ran to the front porch. "He was supposed to get back from Taiz this morning." I yelled into the house. "Kevin!"

Nicolaus rushed after me. "They haven't gotten back, but I'm sure they're fine, Audra. Johnny is driving. He's been through this kind of thing before."

I threw my hejab and my balto at the coatrack inside but missed. Both pieces of black slithered to the floor. "Jack, baby, Mommy's home!" I called. "Jack!"

I turned back to Nicolaus. "Do they know about the riot? They're going to drive right into it."

"We're praying that they won't. Hopefully Johnny will hear about it and take a different route. We haven't been able to reach him on his cell." He sighed and shook his head. "I'm just glad you're safe. Your language helper lives near Tahrir, doesn't she?"

I nodded. "Yeah, right down the street. But what about Madison and Jaden?" My hand went to my throat. "Their bus is due in an hour and a half. They can't drive through the middle of a riot. That bus is filled with foreign children."

Nicolaus chuckled. "In an hour and a half this will all be over. The men will stop to eat lunch and chew qat."

Then his face sobered. "The president has called out the army. They're setting up positions at every intersection."

"Mommy! Mommy!" Jack ran to me and grabbed my legs, dropping wooden blocks to the floor.

I steadied myself to keep from falling. "Hi, punkin!" I picked him up. "Did you have a good morning?"

"Yeah. But Rose wouldn't let me play outside." He poked out his lower lip.

Our housekeeper, Rose, appeared from the kitchen. She had changed her flip-flops to street shoes but was still in her faded work smock. "Bad trouble today, missus," she said. "Not good in the streets. Maybe I wait one hour before I ride *debab* [minibus] home."

"Yes, Rose. You should," I agreed.

The crowded minivan debabs stopped at Tahrir on their taxi routes through the city. "It is better that you wait. You can eat lunch with us and take your rest for as long as you need."

A loud clanging jarred the gate, striking a tingle down my spine. Rose's eyes grew wide. My arms tightened around Jack. Nicolaus's eyes pinned mine, but he said nothing. A man began shouting outside the gate. I could not make out his words. The clanging grew to a loud bang that made the gate shudder in its hinges.

"Audra! Let me in!" It was Kevin.

I thrust Jack at Rose and tore out of the entryway, losing a shoe as I ran to the gate. "Kevin! You made it through!"

I slid the bolt from the gate and threw my arms around his neck. He hugged me, pushing me back into the yard as he bolted the gate behind us. The shouting and banging had faded in the distance.

He grinned. "Lots of excitement around here!"

I linked my arm tightly through his as we walked back toward the house. "There was a riot in Tahrir," I said. "I was afraid you'd drive right into it."

"We knew something was up. There were tires burning in the street when we drove into the city." He held my arm as I bent to retrieve my shoe. "When we saw the smoke, Johnny took the back roads. We were fine on those. Nobody was around."

"Yeah, everyone was at Tahrir," I muttered. "I hope Madison and Jaden make it home okay."

"They should be fine coming from the school. The streets are deserted in that direction." Kevin dropped his arm from my waist as we filed through the door.

Jack ran to him, scowling at me for passing him off to Rose. He nestled his small, blond head under Kevin's chin. Nicolaus was on the phone.

"Well, I think the worst is over for today." Nicolaus said as he replaced the receiver. "Emma said the streets are empty near our house. The crowds left after the soldiers fired tear gas. It sounds like everyone has gone home to chew qat."

Nicolaus smiled and ran his fingers through his salt-and-pepper hair. "Good old Yemen," he said. Then he frowned. "It's probably better to stay in for a few days, though. Foreigners are a target during things like this to use as leverage against the government. You know how Yemenis love to take hostages."

Kevin laughed. "Great ministry opportunity! A chance to visit remote villages."

"Yeah," I added dryly. "Think how our Arabic would improve."

Nicolaus grinned. "I can think of easier ways." He put on his jacket. "Seriously, be careful. If you need anything or something happens, call me."

He looked back over his shoulder. "These are the times we just have to trust the Lord."

"Oh, I trust Him," I yelled as he walked out the door.

Kevin followed Nicolaus to the gate with Jack still in his arms. As Kevin opened the gate, I heard the children's bus pull up.

I twirled a strand of hair in my fingers and looked at my satchel, full of language notes. I chewed my lip. Fatima relied on our Arabic lessons. It was the majority of her family's income. If I did not go for a lesson, she would not get paid. I sighed and looked out of the window at the still blue sky.

"I will trust You, Lord," I said aloud. I left my bag where it was and hurried to greet my children.

It was three days before I ventured to Fatima's house. The city had become smothered by the military. When I finally stepped out of our iron gate, I saw a beige jeep with no roof sitting at the end of our street. A gray machine gun was straddled on its flatbed, guarded by two soldiers in camouflage who were chewing qat. Their AK-47s swung lazily at their sides as their arms reached back and forth for the qat leaves stuffed in a black plastic bag.

"*Sabbah al-kher* [Good morning]," I murmured, moving in front of the machine gun's long nose. I peeked inside it before crossing to the other side.

Soldiers stood shoulder to shoulder on the cobbled sidewalk, crowding it in a thick, long line. Their guns were thrust forward on the bricks like they were ready to churn them into butter. I stared at the plastic shields across their faces and chests and saw myself mirrored in them. I chuckled as I passed just inches from their machine guns. *One day I am going to tell my grandchildren about this*, I mused.

Soldiers roamed every street. Rattling old taxis crept through alleys where people stood in shadows.

I felt like I had been hiding, too. I had paced our floors until I had counted every tile. I had re-read books and replayed games with the children until we all had grown tired of them.

"Lord, I have got to get back to Fatima," I had prayed. Then I had called Nicolaus.

"I can't wait any longer, Nic," I had said. "Kevin has his lessons at home, so he'll be here with the kids until they go back to school next week. But I need to get back to language study." Then I had chuckled. "The Lord is my Light and my Salvation. Whom shall I fear? I trust Him, Nic. He'll take care of me."

And now I was on my way to Fatima's house, content to trust God. Or so I thought.

Fatima's worried frown eased into a wide smile as she pulled me inside her door. She hugged me three times before allowing me to remove my shoes. "I am happy you are here! It has been three days!" she said.

The baby was crying in the living room. I put my shoes on the rack next to hers and unsnapped my balto. "How have you been, Fatima?" I asked. "How is Qasar?"

She grimaced and rolled her eyes. "I am tired. Qasar is crying all the time. My ama [paternal aunt] says he is not eating enough."

"How is your ama?" I asked cautiously.

She answered slowly, as if she disbelieved her own words. "She came and cooked in my house and cleaned my kitchen. Can you believe it?"

"Your mother-in-law?" I was astonished. "*Sahee?* Al hamdulilah! [Really? Praise God!]"

"Yes, she is proud of her grandson. But she thinks he cries because he is hungry. She said the milk from me is not good. I give him the powdered mix now." She looked down at her hands.

I picked up the wailing baby from the mufraj. His thin black curls were wet with hair oil and perspiration.

"Shh, shh, Qasar," I kissed his damp cheeks and patted his padded bottom. The blue jumpsuit I had given him hung loose and baggy. "It's all right, sweetheart. Your *hala* [maternal aunt] Audra has you."

Qasar continued to wail. Fatima shook a painted tin rattle in front of his face. "*Bas,* bas, Qasar! Enough, *habibi* [my love]."

We sat on the thin mufraj. Qasar's wail softened to a whimper and then to a few soft shudders as he slowly succumbed to sleep. I laid him gently between us on the mufraj.

"Al hamdulilah," Fatima sighed.

She raised her hands upward, shaking them hard at the ceiling. "*Al hiyat taub!* [The life is tiring!]" Her frustration spewed like steam from a pressure cooker. She seemed caught, exploding from the pressure but unable to be free of the cooker.

I reached out and touched her arm. "He won't be like this forever," I said. "He is only two months old. Is he eating well?"

"He drinks slowly." She looked at the sleeping infant. The tension in her eyes softened only slightly. "My friends say I should give him biscuit and tea."

"He is too young, Fatima," I countered. I had seen women spoon cookies mashed in hot tea into the mouths of their newborns.

"If you are not nursing him, then he only needs formula. Maybe you should try a different one. Some babies have allergies to some formulas. Have you asked a doctor about this?" I immediately regretted asking.

"The doctor said ensha'allah he will be strong and healthy." Her voice was a monotone. "He said I drank cold water when I was pregnant. That is why the cord wrapped around his neck. The doctor said that is why he cries." She glanced down at her hands again.

I gritted my teeth, wishing I had accompanied her to the doctor. There were things I would have said to him.

"Fatima, that is not true. It was not your fault." I lifted her eyes to mine. "The doctor is wrong, Fatima. American doctors would not say this."

Her eyes searched mine, and she smiled a little. "Audra," she paused. "I want to take him to my family in Aden." She straightened the band on her ponytail. "They want to see him. Maybe there he will not cry so much. Maybe he will get better."

I waited for her to continue. She looked at me and looked away. "The trip is long, more than five hours. Ahmed cannot go with me, and I cannot travel alone." She smiled tentatively. "Audra, will you go with me?" She was almost whispering.

I tried not to show my surprise. "Me? When?"

"After one week. Now it is not too hot."

"In one week? That is soon." I thought of my children. I had been away from them overnight only once before. "I don't know, Fatima," I hesitated.

"Please," she urged. "I must see my sisters, but I cannot travel alone."

I sighed. I longed to be inside a Yemeni home for more than an afternoon visit.

"I could not stay long," I said cautiously.

"One week only." Her eyes were pleading.

"Maybe. I will ask my husband."

She clapped her hands with excitement. "I will tell my sisters we are coming."

"Fatima!" I exclaimed. "Wait! How do you know my husband will say yes?"

She smiled. "Because you are Amrekia [American]."

A week later we were on the bus. The security guard in his olive green suit almost passed my seat as he walked down the aisle to check tickets and travel papers. To him I was every other black-shrouded woman. But I made the mistake of glancing up as he passed, and my blue eyes caught him. He whirled around and asked for my passport.

I handed it to him grudgingly. I knew he would add it to the roster of foreigners traveling in the country. Security forces maintained surveillance on all foreigners and their activities. Some of it was for the foreigners' protection.

I smiled at the alarm in Fatima's eyes. She jostled Qasar in her lap and started to protest as the man walked away with my passport.

"He'll bring it back," I assured her. But I was annoyed. I had wanted to blend in and be insignificant, like any other Yemeni woman.

After the guard returned my passport and the bus pulled away from the curb, a steward passed out bottled water, mint candy and green plastic bags. I returned my passport to my purse and tucked the green carsick bag into my seat pocket, chuckling. "That is not encouraging."

Fatima nodded. "The roads through the mountains are difficult. Many curves." She bit her lip. "I get sick in the travel," she admitted sheepishly. "Do you have medicine?"

I immediately reached for my purse. I handed her a tube of motion sickness pills. "Have you taken this before, Fatima? Are you allergic to it?"

She gratefully took the tube. "These are good," she said. She opened her water and swallowed two pills.

I soon regretted giving Fatima access to more than one pill. Within thirty minutes she was fast asleep. She did not stir for the three hours that Qasar wailed. She never moved during my multiple attempts to soothe him. She missed hearing the man who threatened to harm the driver if he did not stop the bus. She slept through the driver's laughing refusal and the man's subsequent upheavals into his green plastic bag. She also missed the smells as other passengers followed suit.

I fanned my face with the book I had hoped to read and rocked Qasar until his screams finally softened into exhausted sleep. A gory American horror movie played on an overhead video screen. I turned away to look out of the window.

"Lord, help me get through this," I sighed and practiced reading Arabic billboards. It was a long trip to Aden.

When we finally arrived and stepped off the bus, the heat sucked away my breath. Within seconds sweat trickled down my chest.

"It's hot." I wiped my forehead on my balto sleeve.

"Yes, but it is cooler now. In the summer it is quite hot."

I nodded. Compared to the low seventies we had left in Sana'a, Aden seemed hotter than its humid 95 degrees. But I knew the coastal summer could top 115, so I tried to be grateful.

We flagged a taxi to Fatima's house. I lugged our duffel bags while Fatima carried Qasar, who was still sleeping. We arrived at a two-story row house, painted the same peeling yellow as the houses on either side. We opened the rusted gate to a tiny courtyard shaded by a gnarled tree that dripped yellow leaves into a dry stone fountain.

"*Ahlen!* [Hello!]" Fatima called.

The scarred wooden door flung open. Three women stood behind it, straining around each other to see us. With wide smiles and gleeful shouts, all three fell upon us. I was smothered by gripping hugs and profuse kissing. Qasar blinked in a sleepy stupor.

The eldest and widest of the three sisters was introduced as Aisha. She wiped damp hands on her cotton housedress and took Qasar from Fatima. She cradled him in kisses and disappeared into the house ahead of us. Fatima and I followed in the vise-grip of the other two.

Inside a small living room, we took off our baltos and hejabs and sat on a fraying blue mufraj. Yasmine, the youngest of the three, sat with us. She was beautiful with bright eyes that flashed and thick black hair clasped at the nape of her neck. She was wearing a peach rayon dress so wrinkled that I wondered if she thought it was fashionable. Yasmine held Fatima's hand, asking questions too quickly for me to translate.

The shortest of the sisters, Zahra was twice the width of Yasmine but not as large as Aisha. She had sad eyes and gray peppered hair. She smiled and took my face in her cool hands. She kissed my cheeks repeatedly before moving to slide a large white fan into the room. She placed it to face us a few feet away and turned it on high. I gripped my ponytail to keep it from whipping across my face and tried to follow Zahra's Arabic. I responded to her questions while trying to keep hair out of my mouth.

Aisha returned from the back with Qasar, who was asleep again. Wisps of graying hair escaped from the bun knotted on the back of her head. She was frowning. Her light brown eyes were fixed on Fatima. She sat heavily on the floor, covering the baby with a thick fleece blanket as a shield against the fan. Worry rippled across her face.

"He is so thin, Fatima. What is wrong with him? Is he eating?" Aisha asked.

Fatima had not told them about his birth. I waited for her to explain what had happened and how far he had come from his critical first days, but she did not. She gushed light prattle, holding her chin high as she talked. I said nothing.

Aisha jiggled her legs as Qasar began to stir under the hot blanket. "Bas [enough], bas, habibi [my love]. Bas," she crooned.

"Ma'a sha'allah [What God wills]," Zahra whispered. "Ma'a sha'allah."

The doorbell buzzed from the front of the house. Zahra ignored it as she squeaked a toy in Qasar's face. His fretting developed into a fussing cry.

"Bas, bas," Zahra said firmly, repeating, "Ma'a sha'allah," as she kissed the baby's damp forehead.

The doorbell buzzed again. Qasar's cry evolved into an angry scream. "He is hungry," Fatima explained to her sisters' worried looks.

She rummaged in the diaper bag for a clean bottle.

"I will feed him." Aisha rose to take the formula, but Fatima held it away. Clutching it close, Fatima gripped her wailing son and pulled him from her older sister.

"Asalam alaykum. [Peace be upon you]." A woman entered the room and handed her heavily embroidered balto to Yasmine, who had answered the door. *"Kaif halikum?* [How are you all?]"

Her words were scarcely louder than Qasar's wails. She made her way to each of us, kissing our cheeks twice before mopping the perspiration from her face with a wadded tissue. She thumped heavily down in the space Fatima had left behind.

Fatima smiled apologetically as Qasar screamed. "I must feed my son," she told the woman and left the room. Aisha frowned.

"His cry is strong, ma'a sha'allah." The woman nodded approvingly. Then she turned to me. "What is your name?" she asked.

"Audra," I answered. "And you, what is your name?"

"*Om* Hamid," she responded, dabbing the soggy pink tissue again.

I cringed, regretting how easily I had given my name. I had forgotten that a woman's personal name was not freely distributed. It was considered disrespectful. In public a woman was referred to as the wife of someone or as the mother, om, of her eldest son. I should have responded, "Om Jaden," until I knew the woman better.

Yasmine saw my discomfort. "Audra has three children, she told Om Hamid. "Two sons and a daughter."

The woman nodded approvingly. "Ma'a sha'allah." Qasar wailed in the background. "Ma'a sha'allah," she repeated softly.

"Does the baby always cry this much?" Aisha asked, her face a wave of concern.

"Ahyanun [Sometimes]," I answered, thinking it best not to add, "You should have heard him on the bus."

"I think he has colic," I explained.

Om Hamid asked Aisha a question I did not understand. She asked if they had done something to the baby. "What does that word mean?" I whispered to Yasmine.

"It is a special pouch with writings from the Holy Quran and special herbs to keep away the Evil Eye," Yasmine explained.

"Oh, those." I kept my voice even. I had heard about the pouches mothers trusted to protect their infants. Without them compliments could not be given. But with the tiny pouch dangling from a cord around her baby, a mother felt confident that her child was safe from the Evil Eye. She could proudly receive praises for her baby without fear.

Fatima returned to the room with a half-empty bottle and a contented Qasar sleeping in her arms. She squeezed between me and Om Hamid on the mufraj and tossed a sideways glance at Aisha.

Om Hamid began a volley of admonitions. "You must feed your son biscuit mashed in tea. It will make him fat. And stir honey in his milk. It will make him strong. Ma'a sha'allah."

"You must feed him many times in the day, even when he is not crying," Aisha scolded. "He is too thin."

"And put honey from Zabid into his water," Zahra added. "It will give him good health."

"No, Fatima," I whispered in English. "Babies should not have honey. It is dangerous for them when they are small."

Fatima took each comment, including mine, with a tolerant smile. But she rolled her eyes when we took our bags upstairs to our room later. We would sleep in the room she had slept in as a child. It was tiny, with twin iron cots, a small cupboard spilling over with clothes and a sliver of yellowish rug. A single window with a rotting seal was open and unscreened. It was next to a warped door that led to the flat cement roof, where laundry baked on a wire clothesline.

"My sisters think I am their baby still." Fatima scowled. "They think they must take care of my baby and me. I thought it would be different."

She frowned as she fanned herself with a square of cardboard. "It is hot," she said.

I agreed. "Maybe we can bring the fan upstairs?" The room did not have a ceiling fan, which was good since I could touch parts of the ceiling with my hand.

Fatima wiped her face and neck with the hem of her orange dera. "I have become spoiled in Sana'a." She grinned ruefully. "This was my home, but now I do not like the heat." She wrinkled her nose. "Who can sleep in this heat? Qasar will be crying all the night."

I thought about the women who were passing him around downstairs. I did not think the heat would be the problem.

Fatima sat up abruptly. "Wait. Mabrooka has a flat with an air conditioner. She spends most of her time in Taiz. Maybe we can sleep at her flat."

"But your sisters are expecting us to stay with them. Won't they be offended?" I asked.

Fatima shrugged. "I will explain to them about the heat. They will understand."

I realized whom Fatima would say could not tolerate the heat. "Fatima, I can sleep here. *Mosh mosh kila* [No problem]. I am fine." I knew Fatima would use a foreigner's discomfort rather than her own to appeal to her sisters.

"Please, Fatima," I repeated. "I don't want your sisters to think I don't want to stay with them."

Fatima had made up her mind. "After maghreb we will go into town. Then we will sleep at Mabrooka's house."

I hesitated. Sweat trickled down my damp T-shirt. The prospect of air-conditioning was appealing, but I did not want to be the reason we needed one.

As the maghreb prayer call deafened us from the mosque one block away, Fatima, Aisha, Zahra and I sat on the rug in the living room around the supper we had purchased from a nearby mata'am. *Foule* [spicy beans stewed with onions, tomatoes and peppers] steamed in a bowl on the aluminum tray beside a stack of hot khobz [flatbread].

I bowed my head and prayed softly in English. Aisha and Zahra watched curiously. They said nothing, waiting for me to finish.

"We thank God before each meal we eat," I explained to my onlookers. "We want to honor Him for providing food."

Aisha nodded. "Tamam [good]." She gestured for us to begin. We tore pieces of bread and dipped hungrily into the beans, leaning aside for Aisha's three children to have their turns.

I tried to eat sparingly to allow all an equal share. "Eat, eat!" Aisha urged me, glaring at her children to back away until I had scooped again.

We ate together from the blue melamine bowl until the last drop of beans and the last flake of bread were gone. The children licked their fingers. Aisha gave them a small bag of cheese curls to share and sent the younger two outside to play. She handed the tray to her nine-year-old son to carry back to the restaurant while she settled herself on the mufraj with Qasar.

Fatima and I splashed tepid water on our faces and arms and brushed our hair. I was surprised when Fatima kissed

Qasar and almost eagerly handed Aisha the diaper bag. I wondered if she had given in to her older sister's authority.

Fatima grinned and pulled my arm. "We will go to town by ourselves!" she exclaimed. I grinned back as she seized her opportunity for freedom.

We covered ourselves in our stifling black drapes and went into town.

The sun was yielding to dusk, throwing streaks of orange and pink across the sky as it slowly succumbed to the dark. Fatima and I strolled arm in arm through alleys lined with bulging carts and noisy vendors. We entered a muddy square crammed with wooden carts stacked high with clothing, fruit, housewares and shoes. Men, women and children mulled in and out between them. Bare lightbulbs dangled on electrical cords overhead.

"I am hungry." Fatima pulled me toward a boy on a bicycle with a mounted glass box.

I gave the boy money and watched him roll two cones from a stack of notebook paper. He filled each one with hot fries and sprinkled them with salt, drizzling hot sauce on top. We thanked him and ducked into a secluded corner to eat. We licked our fingers discreetly and tossed our empty wrappers into an overflowing garbage bin.

We continued our way through the carts, ignoring the calls of the vendors. The alleys had been hosed with water. We stepped carefully between puddles, avoiding rotten fruit and discarded garbage. We stopped to admire bolts of fabric. Fatima sighed over crinkled red satin. I uncovered pale blue cotton printed with American flags and chuckled at finding it there. We continued our stroll.

Suddenly Fatima stopped and gripped my arm. She scowled at the cart in front of us. Her soft face went hard as she clenched her teeth. Her eyes looked both injured and fierce.

"My husband buys films from carts like these." Her words were clipped.

I looked at the stacks of videos and discs, amused to see current American hits reproduced on the alley cart. "You do not like films?" I asked, not comprehending her disgust.

Her eyes sparked. "Not these films, Audra," she snapped. "Other films. They are hidden. You must ask for them so the police will not know."

She looked at me, anger burning in her eyes. "Films of women," she spat out.

I understood. "Oh," I said. "Those kinds of films."

My heart flinched to see her pain. "I am so sorry, Fatima," I whispered. I slipped my arm around her shoulders. I did not know what else to say.

"Why, Audra?" she asked, hurt rising in her voice. "I told Ahmed that it is harram [forbidden]. But still he does this."

Her eyes filled with tears. "He watches them with his friends. They are husbands! They have good wives! Is this what husbands do? How can we trust them to take care of us?" Her pain choked her words.

I took her arm and led her away from the cart. "No, Fatima. This is not what husbands should do. It is wrong."

I handed her a tissue. "Fatima, it is not your fault that he does this," I said firmly. "It is your husband who is doing the wrong. Not you."

Tears slowly trickled down her smooth, olive cheeks. She wore no makeup, not even lip gloss. Her husband forbade her to wear it in public. I had seen him make her wipe it off when she left parties. He would not let his wife appear beautiful to other men, this man who watched pornographic films.

Anger gritted my teeth. *Kevin stands proudly when I look my best,* I thought. *These men cover their wives' beauty to keep it for themselves. But even that is not enough, not even with the four wives they are allowed by Islamic law.*

Fatima wiped her eyes with the tissue I offered and quickly glanced around at the families weaving in and out. "*Tiyeb* [Okay]," she said. "Khalas [Enough]."

Her eyes caught sight of a man on a white bicycle trolley. "Ice cream," she said, tossing her tissue to the street. "Come!"

I grimaced at the tissue soaking up mud, but I nodded at the cart. "Ice cream is always good!" I agreed.

8

Seven of us gathered at Mabrooka's apartment. Zahra, who was childless and divorced, remained at the house with Yasmine, who was still single. The humid night air hummed with cicadas and the occasional screech of a bird I did not recognize. We were on the outskirts of the city. The constant honking of cars and trucks had given way to a braying donkey and barking dogs. Fatima and the children were as anxious as I was for Aisha to unlock the door. Dripping with sweat, we hovered around her, eager for the air-conditioned bedroom.

I was grateful for Mabrooka's absence. She was the sister of Aisha's dead husband and was also the sisters' first cousin. Mabrooka's husband had divorced her because he found divorce cheaper than maintaining two wives. Mabrooka spent most of her time in Taiz, a four-hour drive away, and she left her apartment key with Aisha when she was gone.

The apartment was one of several built side by side in a one-story row, each with a cement pad as a courtyard. The courtyards were separated by tall iron fences that matched the white iron bars on the windows. Most of the windows were dark.

"*Mabrooka* means 'congratulations,' doesn't it?" I asked Fatima.

"Yes. It comes from the word for 'blessing,'" she said.

I inwardly thanked Mabrooka for the blessing of an air conditioner. Aisha unlocked the door, and we followed her inside. Hot air burst in our faces like a cloud of steam from coals in a sauna. The apartment had not been opened for several days. The heat had been stored inside, waiting to vent on anyone who opened the door. I wiped my face.

We made our way quickly to the room with the air conditioner. Aisha lagged behind to open the screened windows. The bedroom was large and long, lined on one wall with a king-sized bed and a twin bed, and on the other with a triple pine wardrobe. A red paisley rug covered part of the ceramic-tiled floor.

We found the light switch and turned it on. Fatima laid her sleeping baby on the large bed. Aisha's children curled up on the rug and promptly went to sleep on the floor.

Fatima walked over to the air conditioner and studied the switch. I eyed it, trying to be patient. I could almost taste cold air. Fatima found the right button and pushed it. The air conditioner sputtered and groaned. It tried to blow and moaned in its attempt, but then it was silent. I swallowed.

Aisha came in to help. She switched the power off and on, unplugged the cord and re-plugged it. Then she tried again. The air conditioner groaned and shuddered but was silent again. My mouth felt dry. I had been prepared to sleep in Fatima's bedroom without a fan, but then I had been offered refrigerated air. It was difficult to give it back.

It was almost eleven. I was ready to curl up on the rug with the children. I was hot, sticky and tired. The house in which we had hoped was hotter than the house we had left. Fatima looked even more disappointed.

"At least Qasar is sleeping," I said.

"But this heat! Who can sleep in this?" Exasperation cracked her voice.

Aisha went to the phone and dialed a number. Her Arabic was too rapid for me to interpret. She went from gentle pleading to outright scolding the voice on the other end. She reminded me of women bargaining for underwear in the suq. I heard the word *agnabiya* [foreigner], and I knew I was the reason for the distress call. I rolled my eyes.

"Tiyeb [Okay]." Aisha clicked off the phone and turned to us. "The neighbor's husband is coming. He will fix it."

The doorbell rang almost immediately. I reached for my balto and hejab, as did Aisha and Fatima. Aisha welcomed a man wearing a crooked white T-shirt and a hastily wrapped *futa* (wrap skirt) that looked close to becoming unwrapped.

The man held a handful of tools, greeting us with sleepy eyes and a gritted hello as he walked past us to the air conditioner. He grumbled a response to our greetings and went to work. Within minutes the air conditioner growled out air as it rocked grudgingly against the window. The air was not cold, but it was air and we were grateful. We thanked him profusely, and he nodded, declining the warm soda and cream cookies we offered. He yawned and left our apartment for his.

Fatima and I took the king-sized bed, putting Qasar in between us. Aisha took the twin bed beside us. We left the sleeping children on the floor. We changed into cotton gowns and murmured good nights, falling asleep as soon as we hit the pillows.

I awoke two hours later with my legs on fire—or at least they felt that way. I turned on an overhead light. Tiny red dots covered my ankles and calves. "Bed bugs," I muttered. I rummaged around in my duffel bag.

Fatima stirred. "What is wrong?" she asked, lifting sleepy eyes from her pillow.

Aisha snored, her back toward us.

"Something is biting my legs. Is anything biting you?" I whispered. "I have bug spray."

"No," she mumbled and rolled to her other side. Qasar slept quietly on his back.

I found the insect repellent and doused my legs well. I turned off the light and climbed back in bed. I tried to sleep but could not. I imagined tiny bugs crawling up and down my body. I spent what was left of the night slapping them under the covers.

Morning came to me an hour before it came to Fatima. She and Qasar were sleeping soundly as I slipped out of bed. I stepped over the children, still sprawled asleep on the rug, and went into the hall. Hot air slapped me full force across the face. Even at 7:30 in the morning, the heat was brutally strong.

I found Aisha in the kitchen striking matches, trying to light a burner under a teakettle. "Sabbah al-kher [Good morning]," I called out.

Aisha jumped and spun around. She smiled and reached out to hug me. "*Sabbah annur*. Did you rest well?"

"Yes," I lied. "Thank you for bringing us here. The air conditioner was lovely."

Her smile widened with pleasure. "How did you find the suq last night? How is Aden for you?"

I knew "hot" was not the answer she was looking for, so I replied, "Wonderful. The people are lovely. Aden is very good!"

She grinned as she spooned loose tea into two teacups. She poured boiling water and handed one cup to me. "*Sukkar* [Sugar]?" she asked.

"No, thank you." I pulled packets of sweetener from my pocket. "But I would like a little milk, please."

Aisha frowned and then smiled patronizingly. "In the morning you do not put milk in your tea. It will make you sleep. You use milk in the afternoon when you are resting. It will make you relax."

I was bordering on irritability. I did not like strong black tea without milk, and I could see a tin of powdered milk sitting on the counter. I stirred my tea.

"*Shukran* [thank you]." I sipped my tea, trying not to flinch at the bitterness. I went to the mufraj and leaned back against the cushion to begin my prayer time with the Lord.

Before I had finished Fatima padded into the room. She saw the small New Testament in my lap. "You are reading your Book?" she asked.

"Yes." I nodded. "It is my daily bread. I cannot make it through the day without it."

She looked curiously at me. She glanced at my Bible again and shrugged before going into the kitchen. She returned with a tray of *rootee* [small baguettes] spread thickly with soft cream cheese that the children had fetched fresh from the baqala [grocery store]. I had another cup of tea, this time lightened with forbidden milk. Aisha was feeding Qasar.

After breakfast Fatima washed her arms and legs in the laundry room spigot to prepare for her morning prayers. While she recited them, I took a shower down the hall.

I need not have worried about the absence of hot water heaters. The water tank sat on the roof, exposed to full sun, and it sent water through the taps that was hot enough to scald. I took a quick shower.

I heard voices in the living room and went to join them. Aisha was on the mufraj next to a plump, graying woman who was holding Qasar. A white plastic jug of water sat on the floor beside them next to a tall green bottle of olive oil. Qasar was squirming and trying to fuss. He was naked, kicking his legs and bursting intermittent yowls as the woman took water from the jug and rubbed it sparingly over his head and body. She repeated this with a heavier dousing of olive oil, chanting phrases from the Quran with a rhythmic rise and fall in her voice.

Fatima sat near Aisha. Her face was intent on Qasar. She looked ready to snatch him. I remained by the door, not sure if I would be welcome. After several minutes the woman finished her recitation and bounced Qasar up and down on her lap. She grinned broadly, exposing gums where missing teeth had been. She pinched Qasar's cheek hard and kissed her fingers before handing the crying baby back to Aisha.

"Ma'a sha'allah," she said loudly, a wide grin creasing her caramel face.

Fatima took Qasar from Aisha and tried to comfort him as she gathered his clothes. She fastened his diaper as the women began to speak to her. They spoke rapidly, their tone firm and scolding. I strained forward in the doorway to understand. I caught the words *eib* [shameful] and *zalan* [angry].

Fatima looked down as she dressed her son. She seemed to ignore their harsh words. She busied herself snapping Qasar's jumpsuit. But I saw a tear slip silently down her cheek. She cuddled Qasar in her arms and looked up at me, tears brimming in her eyes.

"They say the God is angry that I named my son Qasar and that is why he cries," she said in English. "They say I should change his name to Mohammed. Then the God will not be angry and my son will stop crying."

Pain pierced my heart and pricked tears to my own eyes as I looked into hers. I leaned against the door frame and swallowed. I tried twice to speak. The eyes of all three women were on me, waiting for my response.

I cleared my throat. "Fatima," I spoke slowly. "God is not like that. He cares what is in a heart. Not what is in a name." I looked at the faces fixed on mine. "God is not like that," I repeated. "You can trust Him."

The old woman glared at me. She did not understand my English, but she knew what I had said. I met her hard eyes with my own steadfast ones.

Fatima thanked the two women and wiped her eyes. She stood and turned to me with her tears changed to bright excitement.

"Audra, the woman put water on him from Mecca. It will make him well. It is water from Mecca!" She kissed the baby and hugged him tightly before handing him back to Aisha.

"He will be better now," she said confidently. She kissed the healer's wrinkled cheek and thanked her again.

"Come." She motioned to me. "We will bring tea." I watched Aisha count riyalls into the healer's hand before I followed Fatima to the kitchen.

Fatima heated the kettle while I spooned tea into teacups. "We must go back to Sana'a tomorrow," she said, pouring hot water.

I was stunned. "Tomorrow? But I thought we were staying a week!"

Fatima shook her head angrily. "It is too hot," she said. "The heat is not good for Qasar. That is why he cries. We will come back when the weather is cool." I nodded blankly, wondering if the weather would ever be cool in Aden.

At noon we returned to the family house. The white box fan again was placed in front of us, and I tightened my grip on my ponytail.

Zahra plumped a cushion and slid it behind my back. "Take your rest," she said proudly. "We will fix for you *sayadiya*."

"Sounds delicious!" I smiled. I leaned toward Fatima. "What's sayadiya?" I whispered.

"Fish cooked the Adeni way. You will like it. *Bis bas* [hot salsa]!" She leaned back against the cushions and closed her eyes. A smile played on her lips as she drifted away in her thoughts. She seemed happy since the healer woman's visit, filled with a new source of hope.

Qasar was fussing in the bedroom. I heard Aisha croon, "Bas, habibi, bas [Enough, my love, enough]. Eat, eat."

Aisha had fixed hot tea, heavily sweetened with sugar and cream and thickened with a mashed wheat meal cookie. Qasar did not seem to like it. I sighed.

Two hours later Zahra appeared in her torn housedress, sweating profusely and carrying an aluminum pan filled with red rice and a circle of small, whole fish.

"Sayadiya," she said proudly, placing the pan on the floor in front of us.

"It looks delicious," I said. I bowed my head to pray.

Zahra and Yasmine waited. When I finished, Zahrah mumbled, "Bismillah [in the name of God]," and motioned for me to dive in. "Eat, eat!" She handed me a large serving spoon.

I scooped spoonfuls of fish and rice, dipping my spoon into the bis bas as they had shown me. "This is very good," I said. "*Momtaz* [Excellent]!"

The sisters ate with me, dipping their fingers into the bis bas and scooping handfuls of rice and fish into their mouths. The children ate between us.

Zahra waved a greasy finger, speckled with rice and tomato pieces. "The children want to know if you will eat the fish head," she said, sucking her fingers. "It is their favorite part."

I patted my stomach. "Al hamdulilah," I answered. "I am satisfied. Please, let them have it."

The children waited for Zahra. "You do not want the head? You are sure?" Zahra asked.

"I am sure," I smiled. "Please, let them have it."

At a brief nod from Zahra, all three children dove for my fish head. Sami, the older boy, won. The girls sighed, waiting to see if other fish heads would be left. Zahra's would not. It was poised in her hand to be sucked.

After the midday meal we rested. Fatima fell asleep as soon as she stretched out on her cot in the upstairs room. I lay on mine and watched a yellow wasp buzz in and out of the unscreened window. It was making a nest in a corner of the low ceiling. A chicken squawked outside in the neighbor's yard. I heard children laughing. After the chicken squawked a second time, a woman began scolding and clapping her hands. The children's laughter stopped.

At four o'clock, we freshened our sweating bodies with hot water from a spigot and combed our hair. Downstairs Aisha was pacing the floor. She was trying to soothe Qasar, who did not want to be soothed.

Aisha's face was a radar of worry lines. "He is not well," she said to Fatima. "He cries too much and eats too little. He needs to go to the doctor."

The relaxed pleasure on Fatima's face was wiped away by a wave of concern. Fatima took Qasar from Aisha and felt his head. "Yes," she said, her voice rising. "He feels hot."

"Fatima," I interjected. "It is hot."

"Maybe he has fever," she said, ignoring me. She looked at Aisha. Both women placed their hands on the baby's perspiring head. "Yes, yes, he has fever. We must take him to the doctor."

Fatima rushed to the mufraj. "I will get my bag."

I grabbed my purse and snapped my balto, trying to keep up with Fatima and Yasmine. They were out of the door before I had wrapped my head scarf.

Qasar was wrapped in blankets like a mummy. I heard his muffled cry in Fatima's arms. I was about to object over the heat but I stopped, astonished to see that Yasmine was wearing a veil. Her sisters, like Fatima, did not.

I looked back at Fatima. "Fatima, you should wait until we are in Sana'a. You could take Qasar to see Doctor Alison. Remember her? She came to see you in the hospital." I was almost out of breath as I tried to keep pace.

"But he feels hot. He has fever." Worry rose in her voice.

"Fatima, the weather is hot. And he is wrapped in a heavy blanket. That will make him too hot." I was panting myself.

Fatima looked at me with surprise, almost stopping in the street. She spoke sternly, jerking her head toward the rustling trees. "There is *rih* (wind)!"

I tried a different approach. "Fatima, wait. Doctors in Yemen give everyone the same treatment, whether they need it or not. They give vitamins and antibiotics. It will not be good for Qasar to take medicine he does not need. Do you understand this?"

Fatima brushed me aside. "If my baby is sick, he must see the doctor." Her worried eyes were not seeing me.

I fell behind as we climbed the stairs to a second-floor clinic housed above a pharmacy. We entered a small room with bare cement floors and two open windows. Four rows of wooden benches were crowded with men, women and whimpering children. A wall clock above a table had stopped at 8:30, probably months or even years earlier.

A woman veiled in white rose from her chair and beckoned us. She listened as Fatima and Yasmine explained their need for the doctor, but her eyes were on me, along with the eyes of every other person in the room. She directed us to the crowded front bench, motioning for two men and a boy to give us their seats. They moved to the sills of the unscreened windows.

"Glissee [Sit]." The receptionist gestured at the empty space. She looked at her watch and wrote the time in the notebook on her table.

We sat, leaning against the slatted back. I smiled at the woman next to me who nodded but did not smile back. She studied me, her eyes fixed on mine as if she were looking for something.

The little girl in her lap moaned softly, her head leaning on the woman's arm. Her cheeks were flushed with heat, but she was shivering under a thick fleece blanket. I wondered if she had malaria, a common and dreaded disease in the coastal areas.

Flies buzzed around a half-empty soda bottle on the floor. An overhead ceiling fan moved slowly but created no breeze. One motorcycle and then another roared down the street outside. A car horn blared as children laughed on the sidewalk.

"Bas, bas," a woman soothed a child crying on the bench behind us.

"Come." The receptionist beckoned to us.

Fatima rose with Yasmine. She giggled into my ear as we left the bench. "It is good you are with us, agnabiya [foreigner]! They will not make a foreigner wait."

I smiled apologetically at the woman we left behind, reaching out to stroke the head of the shivering little girl. The woman did not smile back. She sighed, drifting back into a blank stare.

Yasmine pulled my arm. "I am coming." I tried not to voice my irritation.

The receptionist led us inside a small treatment room and closed the door behind us. The white-coated doctor rose from his stool to greet us. He shook my hand first, then bowed slightly to Fatima and Yasmine, who both began talking at once. He appeared to be in his late thirties. He was thin, with kind brown eyes and curly, gray-flecked hair. He glanced nervously at me as he took Qasar from Fatima and unwrapped him on a vinyl-topped table.

Qasar had been asleep, but he began to fuss as the doctor put a stethoscope on his chest and looked into his eyes and mouth. The doctor palpitated Qasar's stomach and abdomen, then opened his diaper and studied the small tan splat.

The doctor handed the fussing baby back to Fatima. "He has a bacteria in his stool," he said, scribbling a note on a prescription pad. "You must give him this medicine three times every day for ten days."

He handed the prescription to Fatima. "And you must give him one dropper of this every day." He gave her another one. "This will make him strong."

"Will he be well soon?" Fatima asked, the anxiety unveiled in her voice.

The doctor smiled kindly. "Ensha'allah," he said, patting Qasar's head. "Ensha'allah he will grow strong and fat."

Relieved, Fatima cradled Qasar and led our way to the receptionist's table, where I paid for the office visit. Fatima tucked her prescriptions for vitamins and amoxicillin into her purse. We made our way down the stairs and into the street. Yasmine adjusted her veil to cover her face.

"Why does Yasmine wear the veil?" I whispered to Fatima.

"Because she is beautiful. The veil gives her God's protection on the street." Fatima talked absently. Her thoughts were on her infant.

"The bacteria my baby has—is it bad?" Her eyes darted back and forth across mine.

"No, Fatima, it is not bad." I said. "Everyone has bacteria in their stools."

I hesitated. I wanted to tell her that bacteria could be seen only through a microscope, but I was not sure if Fatima knew what one was. I sighed. "He will be okay," I told her.

Fatima stopped. I followed her eyes to a withered old woman shuffling slowly down the sidewalk on the arm of a small boy. The boy stopped to let the woman hold out her quivering hand to a man leaving a honey shop. The woman blessed the man and begged him for money.

"*Muskina* [pitiful]," Fatima whispered.

I reached into my handbag for some coins. "*Aywa* [yes]," I whispered back.

Fatima looked thoughtfully at the blanketed bundle in her arms. "*Lahatha* [Wait]," she said. She pulled fifty riyalls from her diaper bag.

I flinched as I saw the bill. "*Hadtha katheer* [This is a lot]," I protested. It was a meager amount, but large in her budget.

Fatima nodded briskly. "*Daruri* [Necessary]," she answered.

"Daruri," Yasmine agreed, adding a five riyall coin to Fatima's bill.

I waited with a heavy heart as Fatima handed our money to the old woman, who smiled down at Qasar and whispered, "Ma'a sha'allah." I sighed. I knew what Fatima's good deed was costing her, but I grieved more for her reason behind it. Fatima seemed to be grasping at sources to trust, doing whatever she could to earn God's favor for her son.

"I must take him to Sana'a tomorrow," Fatima told Yasmine. "The heat is not good for him. He needs the cool."

Yasmine started to protest, but then she looked thoughtful and nodded her head. "Yes," she agreed. "That is best. You must take him back to Sana'a to the cool."

I said nothing, but inwardly I wondered what Fatima would trust next if the cool of Sana'a wasn't enough. *Well,*

I sighed to myself. *At least I won't be the excuse for shortening our visit.*

Kevin greeted me as I stepped off the bus in Sana'a the next afternoon. Ahmed stood beside Kevin, waiting to help Fatima. I greeted him politely and then grinned big at Kevin, giving him a discreet hug.

"That was a short week," Kevin whispered, kissing my cheek. "I missed you, even though it was only three days."

"It was a long three days," I whispered back. "I'm ready for a vacation!"

"I thought that was one!" Kevin teased as he opened the van door for me.

"A vacation for whom?" I exclaimed.

I waved to Fatima as we drove past. "Ma'a salama [Good-bye]!" I called out.

Fatima was still groggy from motion sickness pills. She waved sleepily back. Ahmed was holding Qasar.

I leaned through the open window, letting my smile fade with the bus in the distance. "I'll bet Qasar sleeps for a while," I muttered. "He screamed the whole way home. In my arms!"

Kevin grimaced. "How'd you rate that privilege?"

"I did not take motion sickness pills." I sighed. "Cool air rocks!" I said into the wind. "Praise the Lord for Sana'a. It was hotter than blazes in Aden."

I looked at Kevin. "I meant what I said about a vacation. I think we should go home and plan one. A real getaway to an island far, far away."

"We can do that," Kevin said. "We're allowed time off after six months of language, and it has been more than seven. I don't know about an island far, far away, though. Where do you want to go?"

"Nassau," I answered.

"As in the Bahamas? Yeah, right!" Kevin laughed. "How about Al Khokha on the Red Sea? There's a new hotel there that's supposed to be good."

"Maybe." I sat up. "Hey—let's do it! Let's go to Khokha. Palm trees and privacy—just our family!"

"Sounds great!" Kevin agreed. "But meanwhile, get ready to be attacked by the kids. They're thrilled you came back early."

"I can't wait to see them, too," I said. "I can't wait to get away and just be together. A real family vacation."

I looked at Kevin. "We need some serious paradise."

"Paradise is good," Kevin agreed, reaching to take my hand. "We can all do with a little paradise."

We pulled into our driveway, and I laughed. Little faces were peeking from the living room window and jumping up and down as we parked the van.

Paradise, I thought. *Lord, I'm ready.*

I felt ready. But God was about to show me that I really was not.

9

"It may not be paradise, but it looks pretty good." I rolled down the window as we entered the hotel compound. "Kids, can you smell the sea?"

Kevin steered the van down a sand-packed driveway. We passed cottages that looked like pairs of fat brick cylinders joined together by a wooden door. Each was roofed with reeds woven like Chinese hats. Concrete walls sheltered private patios behind them, next to beds of periwinkles.

"This will be great!" Kevin exclaimed.

"Yeah. Six whole days!" I answered. "And each room has an air conditioner!"

Tall palm trees rustled over sheets of woven bark tacked to weathered fence posts. The woven walls shielded the compound from goats and sheep and the eyes of village onlookers.

"Look at the date palms!" I pointed to a group of shorter palm trees. "See the dates? They're like big clusters of grapes."

"Can we eat them?" asked Jaden. "I'm hungry."

"Those aren't ripe yet. They're still green. But we might be able to find some in the village."

Kevin parked the van next to a long building walled on the lower half with bricks and the upper half with stained-glass sailboats. We got out of the van and stretched the stiffness from our legs after the six-hour ride.

"I'll check us in." Kevin went into a door marked "Office."

I looked for a glimpse of the sea between the bars of a white iron gate. A small patch of blue-green water sparkled two hundred yards away. "I see it!" I cried. "I see the beach!"

The children huddled around me. "Thank You, Lord," I whispered. "Thank You for sea and sand and fresh, salt air."

We unlocked the door of our cottage and entered a short entryway that led to a center bathroom. The doors to the rooms on each side required separate keys. Kevin unlocked them both, and we tossed our duffel bags under twin cots made of wood with rope rungs. I flipped the switch on the air conditioner. Nothing happened.

"What is this!" I exclaimed.

"Khokha has no electricity, remember?" Kevin set our snack box in the entryway. "They turn on the generator at sundown."

"They turn it off during the hottest part of the day? Yeah, that makes sense."

I wiped my face on my balto sleeve. "Why don't we go into the village to buy our picnic stuff? Maybe the A.C. will be on when we get back."

Five miles away, the Khokha village was a small conglomeration of cement block buildings that looked as bleached and weathered as the palm frond fences between them. We bought cucumbers, oranges and freckled bananas from what appeared to be the town suq, a cluster of four wooden tables huddled under a single thatched awning. A small entourage of children gathered to help us. Older eyes scrutinized us from the shade of a nearby tamarind tree.

We made our way to the baqala [grocery store] sandwiched between barefooted children. They crowded into the store behind us, squeezing us against the counter. The shopkeeper clapped his hands and shouted to shoo them away. Cheeks bulging with qat, he welcomed us. "Marhabah!"

We bought loaves of rootee and triangles of cream cheese as dozens of small eyes peered in through the windows. The shopkeeper lifted Jack high in his arms and kissed both of his cheeks. Jack started to protest, but the shopkeeper handed him a lollipop.

"Shukran [Thank you]." Jack smiled, handing me the sucker to unwrap. Jaden and Madison chorused "Shukran" for theirs as the shopkeeper chatted with Kevin.

Twice as many children had gathered to guide us away from the baqala. Jack gripped my skirt, frowning as small hands reached for his white hair. Madison smiled shyly as girls pushed to be near her. Jaden walked with Kevin. He tucked his head down as if he were walking through a windstorm.

"Mommy, what's that?" Madison pointed to a round, thatched reed awning. "What's that camel doing?" All eyes followed Madison's pointing finger.

"*Zait* [Oil]," a man called from under the tamarind tree. He spat qat-green saliva. "*Ta'aloo,* ta'aloo [Come, come]!"

He sprang from his straw mat and waved us to the awning where a camel walked slowly in a circle. The camel was brown and dusty in his harness, bound to the spokes of a huge wooden wheel that was connected at the center to a giant stone pestle. As the camel walked in a circle, the pestle turned on a massive stone mortar. Oil poured from spigots below into plastic buckets on the ground.

"They are grinding sesame seeds into oil." I pointed to a partially covered cart filled with burlap bags of seeds.

"*Tamam* [Good]?" the man asked, his teeth tinged with green.

"Tamam!" Kevin answered.

We clustered against the wooden rail. The camel ignored us. But the qat-spitting man suddenly grabbed Jack and hoisted him high, placing him on the wheel at the edge of the mortar. I gasped, reaching involuntarily to grab him back.

Jack grinned, his little white head bobbing as he went around on his carousel. I tried not to look at the edges of the grinding stone or the huge pestle rolling next to him. I held my breath, trying to smile as Jack came back into view.

After his third round Jack was finished. "I want down, Mommy!" he yelled. I exhaled my relief.

"Khalas [Finished]?" the man asked. He deftly reached behind the camel for Jack, returning him to my outstretched arms.

After a good night's sleep under powerful air conditioners, we spent the morning playing in paradise. The Red Sea was deliciously cool, clear and salty, and the strip of beige sand was wonderfully deserted. The wind whipped small waves in the water that delighted Madison, Jaden and Jack. They splashed as Kevin swam nearby. I swam, too, wearing the long-sleeved dress and leggings I had made from swimsuit fabric. I grinned at Kevin's whistle.

"At least I can swim without drowning," I said. "I'm not going to sit and swelter while y'all splash and play."

"Yeah, poor women." Kevin looked thoughtful. "You never see them go in the water, do you? They sit in the sun in their black garb watching their husbands and children splash in the water."

After dinner we sat around a white plastic table under the trees. The sky was dark and full of stars. The breeze gently rustled the palm fronds as a string of lightbulbs dangled overhead, spilling enough light for us to play a family game of cards.

Kevin looked at me across the table. We smiled at each other over the sleepy, nodding heads of our children.

"Tamam?" Kevin asked.

"Tamam," I whispered back.

On our fourth morning we walked onto the beach as a fishing boat returned from its long night at sea. Less than thirty feet long, the small *dhow* [traditional Arab sailing vessel] was handcrafted of seasoned wood stained dark from years at sea. An outboard motor was fitted on the stern, and a naked mast stuck up from the middle. Its six sailors were bare-chested and deeply browned. A few wore ragged, unbelted trousers. Most wore the local futas [wrap skirts], rolled tightly at the waist.

The dhow pulled near to the shore, and two fishermen jumped out as a small white truck pulled up on the sand. Men spilled out of the truck bed, rushing to help the fishermen haul the large green net. They formed two lines opposite each other. They braced their legs in the sand and hauled the bulging net, hand over hand, in unison. They strained and pulled like a tug-of-war with the net. They heaved with grunts and shouting, sliding the net slowly forward to gut the sand with a wide, wet trench.

"It's full of fishies!" Jack cried.

We moved closer. The net wriggled with fish of all sizes flapping and flaying inside. When the net reached the truck bed, the men scooped the fish with baskets and dumped them onto blocks of melting ice. The last few were wrestled directly from the net. Then the men who had come with the truck left with it, balanced between fish and ice on the truck bed.

The fishermen dragged the net back to the sea and washed it. They picked out seaweed, soda cans and other embedded debris and stacked the net carefully on the stern. They started the outboard motor and chugged down the beach. About fifty yards away, they killed the engine and secured the anchor, then gathered their meager belongings and held them high over their heads as they swam to shore.

I watched their wiry, brown backs glisten in the sun as they walked away from the water and disappeared into a grove of palm trees. "I wonder if that was a good catch or a bad catch," I said to Kevin as I spread our towels on the sand. "The fishermen didn't seem too excited."

Kevin rubbed globs of sunscreen on his arms. "It's probably just another day's work to them."

"I guess so." I looked at the small dhow bobbing gently on the water. It seemed useless, floating with its outboard motor tilted powerless out of the water.

"Will the fishermen come back?" Madison looked up from the trench she was digging.

"Yes, honey. They'll be back at sunset and fish all night again."

"How can they see in the dark?" Jaden wrinkled his face in a puzzled frown.

"They can't really. They use a lantern like that one hanging on the mast. God gives them light, too: the moon and the stars. They are like a map for the fishermen."

"But what happens when clouds cover the sky and they can't see the map?" Madison studied the boat.

"Well, I guess they have to concentrate on what they can see." I kicked off my flip-flops.

Jaden folded his arms across his chest. "I would fish in the daytime," he said matter-of-factly. "It's dumb to fish in the dark."

Kevin laughed. "But sometimes the dark is when the best fishing takes place."

At noon we went back to our cottage to prepare our patio lunch. I opened a can of Danish wieners, split open small rootee loaves and set out ketchup. We bowed our heads, thanking God for our meal and our vacation. We ate hungrily, gulping down hot dogs and several small bags of local chips.

Madison stood from her white plastic chair and turned slowly toward the patio door. Her food was half-eaten on her paper towel.

"Finished already?" I asked. "Do you want something else, honey?"

Madison did not answer. I turned to look at her. I dropped my cream cheese sandwich, knocking over my water bottle. "Madison, are you all right?"

Her face was tilted down. Her eyes seemed blank, focused on an obscure spot on the floor. Her mouth was jerking, her lip twitching upward on one side of her face. She did not answer me.

"Kevin, she's choking!" I screamed.

Kevin's chair flipped backward to the concrete as he jumped up to grab Madison. "Madison, honey, are you all right?" He jerked her face to look at him.

"Is she breathing?" I shrieked.

"I can't tell!" Kevin yelled back. He spun her around and knotted his arms around her abdomen, jerking sharply upward. Madison did not respond. She seemed limp in his arms.

"It's not helping!" I cried. "Maybe a hot dog's caught in her throat!"

I forced my fingers into her mouth to see if I could dislodge it. Madison was unresponsive.

Jack began to cry. Jaden ran back and forth on the patio.

"What can I do, Mommy? What can I do?" Jaden sobbed, wringing his hands. Jack cowered in the corner of the patio.

"Pray!" I screamed at him. "Pray for your sister!"

"Dear God!" I shouted as I tried to dislodge what I assumed was stuck in her throat. "Don't let her die! Don't let her die!"

I was screaming. "Madison, darling! Can you hear me?" Then I yelled at Kevin, "Go get help! See if there's a clinic near here."

Kevin ran out of the cottage and down the path to the office. He was back in seconds.

"No one's in the office, and it's locked," he panted. "They've all gone to the mosque for prayers. A clinic would be closed, too."

He struggled to keep his tone even as he tried to breathe. "There might be a clinic open in Hays. Do you want to try and go there?"

Madison coughed. She cleared her throat and backed away, looking at us. No longer limp and unresponsive, she was bewildered and frightened. She did not seem to know what had happened.

"My mouth feels funny, Mommy," she said. Tears began to fill her eyes.

"It's okay, baby," I said, pulling her into my arms. "It's okay." I knelt on the doorstep and took her on my lap, gently stroking her back and arms. "You're going to be all right." I tried to still the quivering in my voice. My arms and legs were shaking like jelly. Silent tears gushed down my cheeks, but I hid them from Madison as I held her tightly in my trembling arms.

Jaden came close and leaned over us, wrapping his arms around both Madison and me. Jack joined us, stretching his little arms as far as he could around Jaden's. Kevin watched from across the patio, his eyes glistening as he looked at mine.

"Mommy, my mouth is tingling again." Madison's eyes widened as her voice rose in alarm. She sat forward in my lap, with both panic and pleading in her face.

I rocked her back and forth. Jaden and Jack stepped away, their eyes widening with Madison's. I struggled to hold back tears.

"It's okay, sweetheart. Mommy's right here." I looked at Kevin. "What do we do?" I whispered.

"We can pray," Jaden whispered back, quietly watching. I stared at him. "Yes, honey. We can pray."

We gathered around Madison. Kevin led our prayer. "Lord, please help Madison's mouth to stop tingling. Help us find the help she needs, Lord. We pray in Jesus' name. Amen."

We all looked at Madison. Jack played with his shells, making car sounds as he drove them around the table.

"We can pack up and take her to the hospital in Jibla, but it would be dark before we got there." Kevin said. "They probably couldn't do anything tonight anyway."

"We can't even call them!" Frustration cracked my voice. "The only phone is in the office, and it's locked." I held Madison more firmly. "I wish our cell phone worked here. What if it happens again?"

"I don't know." Kevin shook his head. "I don't know."

He sat down on the other side of Madison and encircled us in his arms. "We'll have to wait for the men to get back from the mosque. We can use their phone and call Jibla."

I nodded, gritting my teeth. I felt like I was groping in the dark. *Lord, help us through this!* I cried silently.

"How are you doing, honey?" I brushed hair from Madison's face and gently massaged her back.

"Okay," Madison whispered, leaning against my shoulder.

We waited on the patio an interminable hour before the men's motorcycle roared noisily back into the compound. Kevin was at the office door before the motorcycle was. He came back twenty minutes later.

"I talked with Lisa in the pediatric ward," he said breathlessly. "She said it sounds like Madison had some kind of seizure. She said to bring her to the hospital as soon as we can, but to wait until morning. We would get there too late tonight. Driving would be dangerous, too. People don't use their headlights, remember? The mountain roads can be deadly."

I nodded and exhaled, realizing I had been holding my breath. "At least we know what to do," I whispered, seeing a faint beam through the storm.

I moved Madison from my lap to Kevin's. "We need to get packed so we can leave first thing in the morning."

After I finished packing I tried to force cheerfulness into my voice. "Y'all ready for some fun?" I grabbed a board game and a package of cookies.

We walked hand-in-hand down the lane to the tables under the trees, as we had done each afternoon. The breeze was no longer light and teasing. It had strengthened into a rough wind. Every move we made on the game board was doubled by the wind. Game pieces blew to the ground, mingling with sand.

"We'll have to put rocks on the cards, won't we?" I laughed. But I did not move to collect any rocks.

"I think the wind won this round." Kevin gathered the scattered pieces and returned them to their box.

Jack left his chair to search for shells to add to his pockets, while Jaden studied a centipede crawling on the ground. Madison sat in her chair, watching a dog sleeping near the dining room door. I leaned back in my chair. The palm fronds overhead were dancing in the wind, rustling like stiff taffeta. Two black ravens, their eyes as sharp as their beaks, studied us from three feet away. They stealthily hopped closer to steal the children's cookie crumbs. I waved my arms and shouted to chase them away.

Madison went to the brown, short-haired dog, offering him a piece of her cookie. She looked like a china doll, delicate and fragile. Her light hair was like a golden cloud as she bent to pat the coarse, gritty head of the dog.

"Not my baby girl, Lord." I clenched my teeth. "Not my baby girl."

Over the next four days we visited two doctors and two hospitals. A kind German doctor at the Baptist hospital in Jibla told us that seizures in childhood were not uncommon. He told us that Madison might never have one again. He patted my hand and sent us on our way back to Sana'a.

On our drive back, Madison screamed out with terror in her eyes. "Mommy, my mouth is tingling again!"

I reassured her that it would pass, reaching back to hold her hand from my front seat. I ignored the pain in my arm as I held it for several hours.

The scene repeated itself the next day. Eyes wide and full of panic, Madison ran to me from her play. "Mommy! Mommy! It's doing it again!"

I held my trembling little girl in my lap and soothed her tears while gently massaging her neck and shoulders. "Mommy's right here, honey." I kissed her cheek. "It'll be over in a minute."

I kept my voice calm to soothe the terror in hers. But my own emotions raged inside me like lava deep in a volcano. I wanted to stop my daughter's suffering, but I could not. I could only hold her through it.

Two nights later Madison's screams cut through the quiet of our fitful sleep. "Mommy! Mommy! Make it stop!" I flew from my bed to hers, struggling to catch the breath I had left behind. Kevin stumbled in beside me, switching on the overhead light.

I put my arms around Madison. "What it is it, honey?" I fought to keep the panic from my voice.

Madison stamped her foot on the floor and rubbed her hand. "My foot's asleep, and it won't wake up!" she wailed. She slapped her foot again on the tile floor.

"My hand's asleep, too, Mommy. It tingles. So does my back. Up and down! Make it stop, Mommy!" Her tears streamed onto her nightgown. "Make them wake up!"

I sat on her bed and pulled her gently into my lap, my eyes locked on Kevin's as I held her.

"There, there, honey," I said, forcing a calm I did not feel. "Maybe you slept on them wrong and they went to sleep along with you! Silly foot! Silly hand!"

I massaged her foot for several minutes and then gently propped it on her bed as I massaged her back along her spine. "Is this where it's tingling?" I asked.

Madison nodded, sniffing. Again my eyes locked on Kevin's. I slowly rocked Madison back and forth in my arms as I rubbed her back. I sang a lullaby I had sung to her as a baby. I fought to keep my trembling voice even. I wiped away tears dripping down my cheeks so that Madison wouldn't see them. I talked calmly, but I was wrestling a whirlwind in my heart. *Help my baby!* I screamed silently at God. *Please make this stop! Why are You letting this happen to her? Why?*

I continued to rock my daughter, singing softly until she relaxed in my arms and fell back asleep against my shoulder. She shuddered once and sighed as Kevin helped me lay her gently back in her bed. She rolled to her side, drifting deep into sleep. Kevin tucked her comforter around her shoulders, bending down to kiss her forehead. Barefoot on the cold tile floor, I shivered.

"You need to get under the covers," he whispered, turning out the light. "I don't want you to get sick, too."

I followed Kevin into our bedroom. "What if something's really wrong?" I asked. "This is getting worse. I don't like this tingling in her spine. I'm worried, Kevin."

Kevin nodded. "Me, too." He climbed into bed beside me. "We're going to have to trust God and try to find better help."

I nodded, but inwardly I was screaming at God. *I do trust You! Why are You letting this happen? Haven't we been through enough? Why, Lord? Why?* And I tossed in anger, wrestling my pillow until dawn streaked light into the inky black of the night.

We saw the only neurologist in Yemen. He introduced himself to us in his Sana'a hospital suite and then hooked Madison to an ancient EEG machine. He shook his head, clicking his tongue as he taped each lode to her head.

"I am sorry about this equipment," he said in perfect English. "It is outdated and almost useless. In Iraq we had better than this."

"Iraq?" I asked, stunned.

"Yes, I am from Iraq." He was busy over Madison's head.

I swallowed and looked warily at Kevin, who had raised his eyebrows. Memories of the wars loomed. *The only neurologist in Yemen and he's Iraqi,* I thought to myself.

The doctor sensed our discomfort. "I am grateful for America," he said, attaching the last electrode to Madison's head. "They helped our country get rid of a madman. Now people like me who had to leave or be killed can go home." We nodded, quietly exhaling relief.

"Cool hairdo." I smiled at Madison, gesturing at the electrodes sticking out all over her head.

"You can probably talk to Mars," Kevin teased.

"Daddy!" Madison's worried eyes began to smile.

The neurologist told us that the EEG revealed an abnormality in the left temporal lobe of Madison's brain. He could not tell us what the abnormality was, but he recommended that an MRI be performed in a place with more adequate health care. He suggested that there might be a lesion. He apologized again for his primitive equipment and gave us the EEG printout.

We reported the neurologist's recommendation to the medical director at our IMB headquarters in Richmond. A regional meeting scheduled in Cyprus was twelve days away. The medical director recommended that we take Madison to a neurologist there. The appointments were arranged for us. We braced ourselves for the possibility of a tumor in Madison's central nervous system and pondered what that would mean to her eight-year-old life.

As we waited for the appointments in Cyprus, I barricaded myself inside our home. I battened down our doors and closed my family inside, shutting everyone else out. I felt like we were bobbing on hostile waters, caught in a storm that raged during the night and seethed during the day. The rage of the storm thundered in every tearful whimper as Madison's tingling continued. But the eye of the storm cracked like lightning inside my seething heart. I was angry with God.

In quiet times alone, I sipped my tea and screamed at God. *Why? How could You let this happen? Why?*

In every chore I absently performed, I ranted. *I trusted You, Lord! Haven't we been through enough?*

In the dark of endless nights, I sobbed uncontrollably. *She's my little girl, Father. Please don't take her away.*

And I flipped through the pages of my Bible looking for the explanation I continually demanded from God.

I avoided my colleagues and I quit language study to stay home with my children. I declined Fatima's invitations to visit friends, explaining that Madison was ill and we would be leaving for medical care.

"Ma'a sha'allah." Fatima whispered. "Ensha'allah Madison will be well soon, and she will be healthy and strong."

"Ensha'allah [God willing]," I responded.

I wanted to see Fatima; I missed her. But I did not want Fatima to see my anger toward God. I did not want to jeopardize the seeds I had planted in her life.

I tried to focus on the Christmas holidays. I overdecorated the house with trimmings from our crates. I played carols and sang them with the children, sounding out a joy I did not feel. I decorated cookies with the children and made paper chains. I played on the floor with Madison and her stuffed animals. I wondered if this Christmas would be her last one with us.

When the day finally arrived, we left eagerly for Cyprus. We flew into Nicocea and took a charter bus to our hotel. Madison's neurological appointments were scheduled for the third day of the conference. We were expected to participate until then. I read the schedule with reluctance. I was disinterested and wanted to skip the sessions and wander the rocky seacoast at the hotel's edge. I went involuntarily to each session smiling at others, but I was not interested in their introductions or in giving my own.

Each morning I met with the prayer group I had been assigned and listened to the women share their needs. I prayed along with them. I told them about Madison and asked them to pray, but I would not reveal my own need for prayer. My hurt was raw and deep, and I would not share it with those who could condemn what they might not understand.

I went through the first day of the conference and into the second, stealing away to the beach during an afternoon break. Salt spray stung my face as waves crashed on the rocks at my feet. Navy blue sea stretched beyond me until it became sky on the horizon. I searched for boats far away, looking for those floundering in the endless blue, caught in waters too deep and dark to navigate. I shivered. The salty wind was sharp and brisk, biting through my thin jacket like a cold, steel blade. I glanced at my watch and trudged back to the conference hall for the evening program.

It had already started. I was late again. Every row in the auditorium was filled with singing people. I searched for the top of Kevin's balding head. I pushed my way through smiling faces to slip in beside him.

"Where have you been?" Kevin whispered, clapping his hands to the beat of the praise song in motion.

"Down at the beach," I mumbled.

Kevin nodded and continued singing, turning back toward the stage. I moved my mouth, but I had trouble singing the words.

The keynote speaker delivered a message on trusting God. I sighed, listening with halfhearted interest. Then the speaker told a story. He described a missionary who had spent her life ministering to the needs of an African tribe. She had given her life to loving and living among the people. But a war broke out, and she was caught between warring tribes. She was taken captive, beaten and raped repeatedly by the very people she had come to serve. From the midst of the horror, she cried out to God, asking why He would let this happen to her.

The speaker shared the clear voice of God's reply. "Do you trust Me enough without having to know why?"

I sat forward in my seat. The room around me seemed to become distant and dim. Faces faded away, and all sound seemed to stop as the question shot toward me like an arrow. It hit clean, straight between my eyes, piercing my soul like a firebrand.

Do you trust Me enough without having to know why?

My mouth felt dry, and I swallowed. The speaker moved on, but I could not. Time had stopped for me. I knew God had asked me the question. It was as if He had drawn a line in the sand, and I had to make a choice. I had to choose whether to cross that line and trust Him completely or stay where I was and struggle through what I did not understand with anger and resentment.

The room was cold, but sweat trickled down the back of my neck. I glanced at Kevin, who was focused on the stage as the speaker wrapped up his message and the pianist moved forward to play. I watched Kevin, seeing him not in his seat but in a hospital bed in Virginia. I remembered the long hours I had spent with Jesus over him. I remembered His sufficiency when nothing else, including me, had been enough.

I thought about Yemen. I remembered my doubts months earlier when I had struggled with the difference between what I believed and what others believed in their religion. God had resolved my doubts and definitively answered my question.

Now He was waiting for me to answer His. *Do you trust Me enough without having to know why?*

Tears began to fill my eyes. God had always been faithful to me, even when I had been unfaithful to Him. He had always been who He said He is; He had never been less.

I lifted my face toward the ceiling, and the tears spilled out, pouring down my cheeks. *Lord,* I prayed. *I trust You. You are worthy of my trust, and I will trust You no matter what. Even when I don't understand why something happens.*

The storm within me ceased. The sun broke through like a clear morning after a night of tornadoes. I crossed over God's line in the sand, stepping across with my heart locked on Jesus. I felt like Peter stepping out of a manmade boat to walk on water with the Master.

I joined Kevin and the rest of the auditorium in the final song. I knew days would come when my focus would shift to the water and what lay underneath. I knew I would probably sink in it, as Peter did. But I knew Jesus would be enough to pull me up and set me walking again.

The next morning my prayer leader studied my face as I joined our small group. "You look happy. Something has changed." Her eyes searched mine. "Did you get Madison's test results back?"

"Not yet." I pulled my chair closer to the center of the group. Our group of five was one of several groups meeting in the hotel lobby. I spoke softly. "I crossed the line."

The leader's eyes grew wary. "What kind of line?"

"The line of trust." I looked around at the women and took a deep breath. "I thought I trusted God completely. But God showed me that I had put limits on my trust. He wants me to trust Him not only when things make sense but also when they don't. He drew a line in the sand between how I trust Him and how He wants me to trust Him. He asked me to cross it, and I did."

The prayer leader's eyes studied mine. "What does that mean about Madison?"

I sighed. "There are things I don't understand and maybe never will. That's hard. Especially with my little girl."

I took a sip of bottled water. "But the bottom line is that I trust God. He is faithful to me. And sometimes, that's all I need to know." I set my water bottle on the coffee table and straightened my shoulders in my chair.

The prayer leader smiled as she reached out to take my hand. She held it firmly in one hand and gently caressed it with her other. "I can see the difference in your face," she said softly. The three other women in our group reached out to touch my shoulders.

"Let's pray right now for Madison," the prayer leader whispered. We bowed our heads together.

Three days later we received Madison's test results and were on a flight back to Yemen. Madison had undergone an extensive EEG followed by an MRI. She did not have lesions in her central nervous system. She had an irregularity in the left temporal lobe of her brain, which caused focal seizures in her mouth area. She was diagnosed with Benign Rolandic Epilepsy of Childhood and was placed on anti-seizure medication. She was expected to outgrow the condition by her teenage years.

We flew with joy back to Yemen. Madison's prognosis was excellent, and so was mine. I had learned to trust God completely, not circumstantially.

I knew God would test me in that trust again. I hoped that when He did, I would take His hand and follow Him farther across that line in the sand.

10

Spring returned to Sana'a. Cream-colored pinwheels leaked perfume from the vine along our wall. Neighborhood children pestered our gate to pluck them for their mothers, who wanted the jasmine blossoms to scent their hair. Mornings were clear and fresh. I wanted to skip down the sidewalks in my balto like a child in a field of wildflowers. We were on the brink of summer—and on the brink of finishing language study.

I was both eager and hesitant to be finished. I wanted to complete exams and evaluations and move from the rank of language student to the status of work contributor. But I was hesitant to leave Fatima. I knew our friendship would not end, but our daily time in language study would. I was not sure I was ready to leave it. Fatima seemed to be on the brink of new life herself, of beginning her own relationship with Jesus Christ.

In the beginning Fatima had not let me mention the name of Jesus. She had joined her friends to deride my Christianity, treating my beliefs as inferior to hers. But that had changed after Qasar's birth. She became interested in what

I believed and asked questions every time we were together. She asked me to pray for her needs and brought me names of sick friends. She believed in my prayer and continually asked me to pray for Qasar, who remained developmentally behind, unable to raise his head or sit unsupported.

One morning Fatima took my *ingil* [New Testament] from my lap and caressed it softly. "Helwa [Lovely]," Fatima whispered. "This Book is hallee [sweet]. I want to know the stories in here."

Her words made my heart pound in my chest. I could feel it in my throat. "I want to tell them to you, Fatima," I answered.

We began to study ten core Bible stories, from the fall of man and his separation from God to Christ's death and resurrection as God's way to redemption and relationship with Him. I asked Fatima to help me learn the Bible stories in Arabic. She helped me write and practice each one. She was no longer afraid of them.

One day Fatima listened as I practiced the story of Abraham offering his son Isaac as a sacrifice. She stopped me mid-story. "It was not Isaac he offered. It was Ishmael!" She narrowed her brown eyes at me. "Why did you change his name in your Book?"

I met her gaze evenly. "We did not change it, Fatima. Our Book says Isaac, the son of Abraham."

I showed her Isaac's name in Genesis. Then I continued the story, leaving no room for a sidetracking debate. I wanted Fatima to grasp the full meaning of the story, to recognize the faith and obedience that God had required of Abraham and the subsequent sacrifice God had provided in Isaac's place. I wanted to prepare her ultimately to understand the Lamb that God had provided in our place to fulfill what He required of us. I finished the story without another interruption.

I closed my Bible and looked at Fatima as she sat next to me on her mufraj. The noonday sun streamed through her new burgundy curtains to streak the wall behind her with rose.

"Fatima," I took a deep breath. "Jesus is the Lamb of God. He is the sacrifice God provided as a substitute for us so that we could walk with God. His blood made us clean before God."

Fatima looked away as she considered my words. A tear glistened on her eyelashes. After a long pause, she whispered, "You have your way, Audra, and it is hallee [sweet]. Your Book is good." She looked wistfully into my eyes and took my hand. "We are more than friends, Audra. We are sisters. But you have your way, and I have my way. We will walk in our ways together."

My heart ached as I looked intently at her. I longed for Fatima to experience for herself what she kept trying to experience through me. She wanted my prayers, my strength and my hope, but she wanted to get them her way. When her way was not enough, she relied on me to provide what she was looking for. She saw the relationship I had with God and wanted it, but she would not accept that Jesus Christ was the only way to have it. She pondered it but then backed away.

"We will walk in our ways together," she repeated softly.

I swallowed. "Fatima, how can we walk together if we are walking in different directions? Jesus said, 'I am the way and the truth and the life. No one comes to the Father except through me' (John 14:6). You know this verse, Fatima. I have told it to you before. If Jesus Himself said He is the only Way to God, then there can be no other way, Fatima. Jesus did not lie."

Fatima let my hand fall from hers. She gathered our mismatched teacups and placed them on her tray. "We will walk together always," she said firmly.

Tears misted my eyes. "Not always, Fatima. There will be a day we cannot walk together."

"Oh, yes, I forgot." Tears clouded her eyes as she looked at the tears in mine. "You are leaving Sana'a," she whispered.

I dabbed my tears with a tissue before they spilled down my cheeks. Fatima would not let me interfere with what she wanted to believe, even if she knew it was not enough.

She stood, holding the tray to take to the kitchen. I stood and took my balto from the coatrack as Qasar began to whimper in the bedroom.

Pain cut through my heart. "Yes, Fatima. I am leaving Sana'a."

At home, I reached to hang my balto and hejab on the coatrack and watched them spill off the hook and wilt into a puddle of darkness. I knelt slowly to retrieve them, feeling like my heart had spilled with them. Tears welled in my eyes. I could not stop them as they poured down my cheeks.

I leaned against the wall. "Lord, I have failed," I sobbed. "All these months I've poured myself into Fatima! I've gotten nowhere. She will not accept You as Savior and Lord." I walked into the bedroom and sat in my rocking chair. I dropped my head into my hands and wept inconsolably.

When my tears were spent, I dried my eyes and looked gloomily out of the window. "Lord, I'm sorry," I said, shaking my head. "I'm sorry I did not do more or say more or use more opportunities. I have failed You."

I thought of Fatima reciting her prayers and performing good deeds, searching for hope that would remain unfulfilled apart from Christ. I leaned back against my chair and closed my eyes. I felt bone weary.

A verse from Isaiah streamed into my thoughts. "The people walking in darkness have seen a great light" (Isaiah 9:2). I opened my eyes.

"Lord, You are the Light." I sat forward in my chair. "You are the Light of the world—Jesus, alive and shining in the darkness. There is always hope in You! Which means there is still hope for Fatima!" Fatima had not yet accepted Jesus, but seeds had been planted. I prayed they would take root and that God would put others in her life to water them.

A few days later Kevin and I joined our colleagues for dinner at our supervisor's home. Everyone clapped as we were awarded plaques for completing eighteen months of language study. "Well done!" cheered Johnny, and Shirley echoed, "Congratulations! You made it!"

Kevin pretended to mop sweat from his face. "I'm just glad we finished!" Everyone laughed.

"So what now?" Johnny asked. "Have you made a decision to work in Taiz or the Tihama?"

Kevin and I looked at each other. "We're still praying about it," I answered cautiously.

Kevin nodded. "The Tihama seems to be where God is leading us, but we need affirmation."

I looked at our colleagues. The Tihama was the western coastal region of Yemen, a region of four million people. It had not had a strong evangelical presence in thirty years. But it was also the region that included Khokha.

"We were in Khokha when Madison had her seizure," I explained quietly. "The children said they never wanted to go there again. They associate bad memories with that area."

Shirley cleared her throat. "We will pray that God makes His direction clear and affirms it in an unmistakable way."

Days later sunlight splashed through the stained-glass *kamariahs* in my bedroom, bathing my floor with blue, yellow and red. I sipped my early morning tea as I read Psalm 139. Suddenly the words "on the far side of the sea" (verse 9) jumped off the page at me. I stared at the page in my Bible. It was as if no other words were there.

Kevin came into the bedroom and sat down on the bed. "Audra," he said. "I've been praying about where we should work. I feel like God might be calling us to the Tihama. What do you think of living in Hudaydah?"

The province capital and the largest city in the Tihama, Hudaydah was only a two-hour drive up the Red Sea coast from Khokha. I looked back down at the words of Psalm 139. "I think that's the far side of the sea God is telling me about." I swallowed. "But what about the kids?"

Kevin raised his green eyes to stare out of the window. "I don't know. I don't want to take them kicking and screaming."

"No, we can't do that," I agreed. "But what do we do?"

Kevin looked intently at me. "We'll have to do a lot of praying."

I put my Bible on the windowsill and nodded. "If that's where God wants us to go, then He will work this out with the kids."

Three weeks later we arrived at our hotel in Khokha to explore and pray about the Tihama assignment. We tentatively exited the van. All five of us stared at the row of prefabricated buildings peeling under metal roofs.

"Is this our hotel, Daddy?" Madison asked. She reached for my hand.

"Not sure I'd call it a hotel," I muttered to Kevin. To Madison I said, "Look! There's a swing over by that sand path. I bet that path leads to the beach!"

A slight smile eased Jaden's grimace. Perspiration beaded on his nose. "I want to go swimming," he said. "It's hot."

"It is hot," Kevin agreed. "This is the hottest time of year. It can reach 120 in the summer." Kevin wiped his face on his shirt. "Visitors avoid the Tihama in the summer. That's why the hotel where we stayed before was closed."

I looked at Madison. She was watching Jack put sun-bleached shells into his pockets. "Can we go swimming, Mommy?" she asked.

"Sure, honey. Let's get checked into our room, and we'll unpack our swimsuits."

Kevin and I looked at the flaking, metal buildings and then back at each other. One long building with screened sides appeared to be the dining room, but nothing was marked with a welcoming sign, and no one seemed to be around.

The midafternoon sun felt brutal. The white buildings seemed to peel in the heat as we watched. Not a single tree shaded them. I looked closer at the wooden swing, which creaked as a thin gust of breeze tried to stir it. It was rusted, and its wooden seat was cracked in the middle.

Air conditioners perched in the small windows of the rooms, but they were rusted brown with corrosion. "I hope those work," I said to Kevin.

"Me, too." Kevin wiped his face again. "Definitely hotter in July than it was in December. I'll see if I can find someone to check us in."

He went inside the long metal building and returned after several minutes. "We're checked into room number three." He grinned. "I had to give them money to buy gas for the generator. They are out of petrol."

I rolled my eyes. "Well, at least we'll have air-conditioning."

Kevin studied the row of crusted air conditioners. "Maybe."

A half hour later we were in our swimming clothes and on the dark gray sand of the beach, which was sprinkled with globs of black tar. "Race you to the water! Watch out for tar!" I dropped Jack's hand and started running. Laughing, we raced into the sea together. But our laughter stopped the minute we entered the water.

"This water's hot!" Jaden yelled.

"Yeah, hot!" Jack echoed, backing out onto the sand.

It was hot. The small beach was part of an enclosed bay with water less than five feet deep. The sun had heated the shallows to the temperature of a spa. It was less than refreshing in the heat.

"Yucky." Madison showed me her handful of muddy silt. "Is this sand, Mommy?"

"Well, it's a kind of sand," I ventured. "Maybe it'll be fun to dig on the shore."

Madison looked at Jack who was running back and forth on the gray sand. He seemed to be the only one delighted with the beach. He was scooping shells into his plastic pail, running from sand mound to sand mound in search of his treasures.

Suddenly Jack stopped. He screamed and threw his bucket to the ground, slinging shells in all directions. His blue eyes were terrified as he raced toward me. "Mommy! Mommy! Help!"

Kevin and I rushed from the water. I reached Jack first and jerked him up in my arms. "What is it, honey? What's the matter?" I searched his small body.

Jack wrapped his arms tightly around me and hid his face. "They're going to get me!" he sobbed.

"Who's going to get you?" Kevin looked around the sand.

"I don't know!" Jack wailed.

Kevin walked over to Jack's bucket and carefully searched the sand mounds around it. "Oh, my goodness!" he shouted. "Crabs! Hundreds of them!"

"Oh great," I moaned.

I kissed Jack's head. "You haven't seen that many crabs before, have you? They probably thought you were going to put them in your bucket, too!"

Jack shook his head firmly. "No more shells, Mommy," he sniffed. "I want to stay in the water."

I kissed his cheek. "Those crabs were more afraid of you than you were of them, honey."

"Can crabs get in the water, Mommy?" Jaden peered down at the brown water around him.

Madison moved quickly out of the water. "I'm tired of swimming, Mommy. I'm ready to go back to the room."

That night we listened to the even breathing of the children squeezed beside us in the double bed. Kevin and I talked in whispers. "Maybe this exploratory trip wasn't such a good idea. Not in the summer anyway," Kevin said.

I could not see his face in the darkness, but I could hear his frown. "We have to make a decision, and it's summer. This was the only time we could come," I reminded him. "Besides, we'll have to face summers if we live here. Might as well know what they're really like." I groaned. "But what a place to do it! How are the children going to change their minds about the Tihama at a place like this?"

"It was the only thing open in Khokha, and we had to come back here," Kevin answered. "They've got to stop associating it with Madison's seizure."

I drummed my fingers on the sheet and started to giggle. "Now they'll associate it with crabs and hot seawater."

"And spiders," Kevin chuckled. "Not every hotel room comes with spiderwebs in the corners!"

I snickered. "Yeah, and makes you buy your own gas for the generator."

"And buy your own water because the cistern ran out," Kevin snorted. "They provide the bathroom, but you provide the running water."

Kevin and I were both shaking with laughter. "Sshh! Shh!" I giggled. "We'll wake up the kids!"

Kevin chuckled again. "And no discount for the room. I guess electricity and running water aren't part of their amenities."

I took a deep breath and let it out slowly. "Well, at least the kids will get a real picture of life here. It won't be sugarcoated."

"That's for sure," Kevin chortled. "The heat has melted the sugar coating clean off."

The next morning we drove to Hudaydah, a seaport city of 450 thousand people, the fourth largest city in Yemen. It was the city where we would live if we accepted the Tihama assignment.

Most of the men in Hudaydah wore futas, a woven length of fabric wrapped at the waist. The women were veiled and robed in black baltos. I straightened my shoulders. *If they can stand theirs in the heat, then I can, too,* I told myself.

We stopped at the fish suq, next to a shipyard crowded with curved wooden ribs in varying stages of completion. Shirtless men strained as they hammered lumber onto the dhows. Their wiry backs gleamed with sweat as they perched precariously on handmade ladders. One dhow stood finished, painted bright red with a border of pink, yellow, green and black.

My eyes were drawn to a row of beached dhows languishing in the background. They seemed forgotten, their barnacled sides unscraped and their holes unpatched. They were listing on the sand far back from their modern sea mates. I wondered how long they had been there.

We moved into the fish suq, a building with four open sides and a wide tin roof that popped and crackled in the sun. Sea creatures of all sizes and species were sprawled on wooden tables and in piles on the cement floor. Blocks of ice melted in a corner. A group of men loaded fish into a few remaining trucks, while others chipped ice to shower over them.

Outside the building on the far end, fishermen bustled on the dock, securing their belongings and hosing down equipment. One fisherman waved us over to see his catch. He proudly displayed three hammerhead sharks, each four to six feet long. We congratulated him and stepped over ropes to view another man's catch. His catch included a shark I had not seen before.

"Jaden, did you bring your book about sharks?" I asked. "Does it have one like this?"

Jaden waved his book and we opened it together, pouring over the color photographs. As we looked from page to page, I glanced up. I was startled to see a cluster of faces surrounding us. Nine boys pushed to get a closer look at Jaden's book. Jaden's eyes grew wide with alarm, and he clutched his book tighter in his hands. The boys pushed closer. I stepped back, pulling Madison and Jack, to give the boys more room. Kevin watched from behind.

Most of the boys were bare-chested. A few wore ragged T-shirts, thin and fraying at the sleeves. All were in torn, faded trousers, some without zippers. Their barefoot feet stuck out from short, ragged hems.

"Jaden, can you hold up the book so they can see it better? They want to see the pictures," I explained.

Jaden raised anxious eyes to mine. The boys were pushing close, crowding all around him.

"They just want to see the pictures, honey," I assured him. I looked at the boys, who ranged from eight to twelve. Their eyes looked hungry, anxious for a glimpse of what Jaden had.

"They have probably never seen a book with color pictures," I added softly. "A lot of boys in the Tihama don't go to school. Even when they do, the schools can't afford books with pictures."

Jaden lifted his book slowly for the boys to see. The boys grinned and nudged each other, pointing and exclaiming over the photographs. One boy reached out and patted Jaden's shoulder. "*Kwoyis* [Good]," he said.

Jaden nodded. He moved his book around the group so that each boy could see it. He turned the pages so the boys could see more. One boy pointed to the hammerhead shark in the picture and then to the hammerhead on the dock. Jaden grinned and nodded.

I looked at the blond, curly head of my son bobbing in the sea of dark ones. Love rushed through me like a wave, surging over my son and these sons of the Tihama. My heart was moved by their hunger to know.

I locked eyes with Kevin over the heads of the boys. A slight smile played on my husband's mouth. I winked, and he winked back.

The next morning we left the hot, dusty coast of Huday-dah and drove high into the verdant mountains of Taiz, arriving during a gentle summer shower. We had agreed to visit Taiz before making our decision.

The air was cool and fresh and smelled like soil and green vegetation. Our colleagues welcomed us with a sa-vory meal of roasted chicken that we ate Yemeni-style on their living room floor. We devoured it hungrily, renewed by the mountain air. Gazing out their window, we were awed by the panoramic view beyond their garden of fruit trees. A green valley stretched wide at the bottom of a giant staircase of ledges planted with narrow gardens.

I looked at the children and chewed my lip. I wondered how they would perceive the beauty of Taiz against the challenges in the Tihama. My mind drifted back to the eyes of the boys at the suq, hungry to see and know more than they did.

"You would like living in Taiz," our hostess told the children. "There are lots of American children to play with. And it never gets real hot, not like it does in Hudaydah."

Madison frowned and leaned toward me. "But, Mommy, I want to live in Hudaydah," she whispered.

"Yeah, me, too," Jaden whispered loudly. "I thought we were going to live in the Tihama."

"Yeah," Jack echoed. "By the beach."

Paula drew back in astonishment. I looked at Kevin, speechless. We had our affirmation.

Our belongings were crated and trucked ahead of us to Hudaydah. I walked through our empty Sana'a house one last time so the children could say good-bye to each room before we locked the door behind us.

"One more stop and we're on our way to Hudaydah!" Kevin called out as we buckled our seatbelts.

"Everybody ready?" I looked over my shoulder and then back at Kevin. "Now comes the hardest part," I whispered.

We headed to Fatima's house, where she hugged me and clasped both my hands in a tight grip. "You will call me? You will visit me when you come to Sana'a?" Her voice was urgent.

"Akeed [Of course]. Remember, Fatima: You will always be in my heart."

She released one hand to touch the silver heart hanging from the chain around her neck. "I will remember," she said softly. "Thank you for this, Audra."

"You're welcome." I studied her face. "Fatima, you must continue Qasar's therapy with Frances. You must do this each week. Please. He won't improve if you don't."

I looked anxiously at her. Frances was a colleague who cared as much about Fatima's spiritual therapy as she did about Qasar's physical one. It was difficult to leave Fatima knowing she still did not know Jesus as Lord, but I knew I was leaving her in competent hands—hands that would water the seeds I had planted in Fatima's life. I moved to the door.

Fatima clung tighter to my hand. "You must call me on Friday," she pleaded.

"I will." I blinked back tears. Fatima slowly let go of my hand as tears filled her eyes. We stood looking at each other.

Qasar began to cry in the living room. Kevin honked the van outside in the alley. Fatima and I sighed together as Fatima rolled her eyes.

"At least he doesn't cry so much now," I said. "He even smiles sometimes."

"But he does not sit up, and he is a year old." Her ever-present worry creased her eyebrows. "Please pray for him," she pleaded.

"I will. And that's why you must work with Frances. Every week, Fatima. And I will keep praying—for him and for you." A tear slid down my cheek as I squeezed her hand again.

"Yes, yes, you must." She hugged me as Qasar's wail turned to an angry scream. She slowly released me, letting me out of the door as she squeezed my hand again.

"Ma'a salama," she whispered.

"Ma'a salama. Ensha'allah, *ba'ashoofik yom thani* [Goodbye. God willing, I will see you another day]." I once more looked her in the eyes and then stepped out into the stairwell.

"Ensha'allah." She slowly closed the door behind me.

I walked down the stairs to the waiting van. Kevin was drilling his fingers on the steering wheel. "Ready?" he asked.

"Yes. A little harder than I thought." I looked up at Fatima's window. She was peeking from the curtain with Qasar crying in her arms. *Thank You, Lord. Keep shining in Fatima's life. Open her eyes to see and know You. Take care of her, Father,* I prayed.

I turned to the children and buckled my seatbelt. "Everyone ready for Hudaydah?" I made my voice sound bright, but it felt hollow in my heart.

Kevin pulled out of the dirt alley. I watched Fatima's curtain grow smaller and smaller in the distance until I could see it no more. I wondered when I would get behind that curtain again.

11

Kevin shivered under the thick fleece blanket I had tucked around his shoulders. His fever had climbed to 102. I held water to his quivering lips, trying not to look at his yellow eyes and pumpkin-colored face.

"Do you want fresh ice?" I asked.

"No, this is fine." His voice chattered with his teeth.

I took his uneaten bowl of soup back to the kitchen and wiped the sweat off my face. It was midday and 110 degrees. I emptied the soup and washed the bowl twice, sighing as I dried it.

The doctors at Jibla Baptist Hospital had assured me that Kevin's hepatitis would not last long. There was nothing I could do but wait. I washed my raw hands again and groaned as Madison cried from her bedroom.

"Mommy, I'm throwing up again!"

I hurried to her room with a wet washcloth, passing Jack who was running to the bathroom.

"Mommy, I have diarrhea again!" Jack wailed.

"I'm sorry, honey!" I hurried past him. "I'll be back in a minute to help you!" I called over my shoulder.

I sponged Madison's face and washed out the basin. "Feel better?" I asked.

"I feel sick!" Madison cried.

"I know, honey." I stroked her cheek. "It will pass soon. Jaden's virus lasted one day, and now he's outside playing. Maybe tomorrow you'll be outside playing, too."

Madison leaned back against her pillow as I smoothed her hair. "Just rest, sweetheart. Maybe a good story will help." I kissed her forehead and handed her a book. "It'll be over soon."

I hurried to the bathroom. "My bottom hurts!" Jack wailed.

"I know, honey. Why don't we run a bubble bath and you can sit and play in the tub? It'll make your bottom feel better."

I put the stopper in the tub and squirted liquid baby wash. I turned on the faucet. A stream of water poured thinly out before it trickled away to nothing.

"Oh great! The water's off again." I slapped the side of the tub as I stood up. "Great timing!" I threw a washcloth hard at the wall.

I was tired. I had spent three endless days caring for sick children and a sick husband. And now, in the middle of intestinal viruses and hepatitis, the city water was off again, an event that had become a common occurrence in the three months we had lived in Hudaydah.

I realized Jack was watching me. "Don't worry." I smiled at his pouting lips. "I'll turn on the pump. We have a cistern full of water under our house. You'll have a bubble bath in no time!"

I went into the outer hall to switch on the water pump. It clicked twice, but the pump did not come on. I switched it off, then tried again. The motor clicked but did nothing else.

"Not now," I growled. I picked up the wrench and tapped the pump gently on the lever as Kevin had shown me when the motor was jammed. I tried the switch again.

The pump no longer clicked. It was silent. I whacked the pump hard with the wrench and jerked the switch. Silence. I kicked the pump with my foot, threw the wrench at the switch and tried again. Nothing happened. The pump was dead.

Tears spewed out as I shouted at the ceiling. "I could use a little help down here, Lord!"

The frustration of the last week boiled over with the frustration of the last three months. We had tried to meet the locals, but they did not want to meet us. We had tried to initiate life-improvement projects, but nobody seemed to want them. Nobody seemed to want us.

I looked at the ceiling again, dabbing my eyes with my T-shirt. "We could use a little help down here!" I repeated softly.

The words of my morning devotion came back to me. "Peace I leave with you; my peace I give you. I do not give to you as the world gives. Do not let your hearts be troubled and do not be afraid" (John 14:27).

I sat down on the step. I had pondered that verse when I had read it that morning. I had wondered what Jesus meant by "not as the world gives."

I trudged back to the bathroom, lugging one of our ten-gallon jugs of drinking water. "We'll use this water," I told Jack, who was sitting naked in the empty bathtub. I poured the water in and sloshed it around with my hand to make bubbles. Jack dumped his bath toys and began to play.

Not as the world gives. I closed the toilet seat and sat down, pondering the Scripture again. Then I understood. Jesus' peace was not the absence of conflict or problems. It was the presence of a Person—His Person, the Prince of Peace, abiding in me.

I smiled slightly, "Okay, Lord, I get it," I whispered. "My mind set on You. That is peace, even when everything else is chaos."

Late that night I e-mailed our families and prayer partners, urging them to increase their prayers. We had faced an onslaught of sickness from the moment we arrived in Hudaydah. The Tihama was an area unreached by the message of God's love. Doors would not open, and the onslaught would not end without strong prayer intercession.

I opened an e-mail from a well-meaning friend. "With all that you are suffering, are you sure you are where you are supposed to be?" she wrote. "Do you think this is a sign that you are not supposed to be there?"

Her e-mail irritated me. I grumbled at the keyboard. "Why do people think obeying God means walking a path of roses? Roses can't grow without broken ground and thorns!"

I typed fervently on my computer, explaining our circumstances and pleading for prayer. I assured my friend that the presence of opposition affirmed the fact that we were exactly where we were supposed to be. I hit the Send button and buried my head in my hands.

I thought about the boys at the fish suq and hundreds more like them we had not yet met. "Lord, there are four million people in the Tihama like those boys, people hungry to know more than they do, hungry to be loved as only You can love. Work in this land, Lord," I prayed. "Move Your mighty hand and draw them to Yourself."

I prayed passionately, longing for the Tihama people to hear and know Jesus. Then, as I prayed I became suddenly overwhelmed as I saw God's power. I saw His ability to move across Yemen as the Almighty God, pouring His love, surging forward to bring His peace and reconciliation to every man, woman and child.

I was ecstatic. "Yes, Lord! Do it!" I cried. "Move forward!"

But then I saw God holding back. It was as if He were standing on the crest of the mountain ready but waiting. He was capable, with every resource at His command, fully able to take over the valley. But He was not moving. He was waiting.

I was confused. "Why, Lord?" I did not understand. "Why are You waiting? You desire that every one of these people be saved and come to know the truth. Your Word says so (see 1 Timothy 2:4)! Why are You waiting?"

I heard the Lord's clear answer. "I am waiting until My desire is the desire in the hearts of My people. I am waiting for My people to want what I want and to ask Me for it."

Tears misted my eyes as the picture faded slowly away. One by one, I closed my program files and turned off my computer. *Did God's people desire Muslim nations to hear God's message?* I stared at my face reflected in the darkened monitor. *Were God's people praying like they desired it? Were they praying like they believed God could do it?*

I slowly walked to the office door and stopped to look back through the uncurtained window. A green neon sign flashed in the distance from the pinnacle of the neighborhood mosque, illuminating the mosque's presence. I stared at it several minutes, thinking about the Light God had sent to illuminate His presence. Yemen had yet to see and understand that the Light is Jesus.

I closed the office door behind me. "There's a lot of work to do, Lord, but it's not going to start in the Tihama." I turned out the lights in the hall. "Our work has got to start back home, calling Your people to pray."

One morning not long after, the sun splashed color through the stained-glass kamariahs as I looked at myself in the mirror. I was wearing the most American outfit I owned: khaki pants and a button-down blouse. I held my balto limply in one hand and my hejab in the other.

"Should I wear them?" I whispered at my reflection with my eyes on the balto and hejab. "What if they get mad and don't invite me back?"

I was about to join a group of American and European women, the only English-speaking women I had met in Hudaydah. I had met them through an American couple who had been in our home for dinner. The couple worked in Hudaydah periodically with a Canadian oil company. Although we had been mutually disappointed in each other's lifestyles, the wife introduced me to other Western women in the city. I had been thrilled by their invitation to join them for a shopping expedition in a nearby village.

But their invitation had put me in a quandary. These women were not personally interested in the local women. Their hired driver drove them where they wanted to shop, answered their curiosity about local customs and negotiated sales for them as needed. They did not wear baltos. In the Tihama heat they wore T-shirts with cotton skirts, bare legs and sandals. They were polite to the locals but were not interested in friendships with them.

I was. But I wanted my English-speaking friends, too. Our family comprised five of less than twenty Westerners living in the entire city of 450 thousand. I was lonely. I had not yet made local friends, and I did not want to lose my new Western ones. If I wore my balto, I knew I could.

The gate bell rang. I hurried outside and climbed into the Land Cruiser. "Good morning," I said brightly.

One woman snickered. "Well, look at you! Good morning."

Another woman murmured a greeting while another said nothing. She scowled at my hejab.

I swallowed and pretended not to notice. "I can't wait to see this village! Thank you so much for inviting me!"

One woman nodded; the other two looked out of the window as we pulled away from my gate. They began to talk about their cocktail party the night before and the unbearable heat of the Tihama. They ignored me. My heart sank.

We arrived at the village, a cluster of mud-brick huts with thatched roofs nestled between small concrete block houses. A small white mosque stood off to the side. Next to it was a one-room building with the black letters *madrasa* (school) fading on its weathered sign. On the other side of the mosque was a well. A pink plastic bucket dangled above its stone-edged hole.

The SUV bumped through a sandy alley and stopped next to an awning made of palm fronds. Two men sat underneath with a large wooden loom between them. We climbed out of the car and walked over to watch.

The weavers nodded to us, neither smiling nor frowning. They faced each other from their cross-legged positions on the ground. One slid the threaded shuttle across the loom to the other, who wove it through and slid it back. They were weaving stripes of red, black and yellow interspersed with slivers of lime green.

The driver explained the process. "They are making two futas [wrap skirts] at the same time. See the open threads in the middle? They will cut them apart when they are finished. Then they will weave a border for the edges. They can make any word you want in the border. If you give them a name, they will weave it."

"Where do they get the colored thread?" I asked in Arabic. One of the weavers looked up.

"Ah, you speak Arabic! This is good!" The driver responded in Arabic. The weavers grinned, nodding in agreement.

The driver continued in English. "The women dye the thread, or they buy it colored." He showed us a basket of thick cotton thread sitting next to the weavers. "When the weavers finish, the women take the futas to the sea and beat them in the water. The salt sets the colors and makes them shiny."

He took a finished futa from a stack and showed us. It looked like polished cotton. We marveled over the craftsmanship.

The Western women purchased several through the driver, who pocketed some of the payment before giving it to the weavers. The women said nothing, as if this had been done before.

I looked down the alley at the row of huts. Each had windows, but none had glass panes. Their wooden shutters were propped open with sticks. Thatched roofs rustled in the breeze over mud houses while corrugated tin crackled over concrete ones.

A movement in the nearest doorway caught my eye. We were being watched. I tried to make out who it was. I noticed movement in other doorways. The village women were watching us, peeking discreetly from the darkness of their homes. I smiled at them and nodded. I saw a flash of teeth as someone smiled back.

The women were exuberant on their ride home. They were happy with their purchases and excited about using the futas as tablecloths. They talked about a village that made pottery and made plans for another shopping expedition. But their plans did not include me. They talked as if I were not there. I swallowed.

When we stopped at my gate, they turned briskly to murmur good-byes. They watched me get out of the car and then drove their SUV out of my life.

I sobbed on Kevin's shoulder. "I wanted so much to have friends," I wailed. "I wanted them to like me."

"You did the right thing, sweetheart." He hugged me close.

"I know. But that doesn't make it easier." I blew my nose. "But still, that village was so cool. They make those futas on an outside loom on the ground. Two guys by hand! I want you and the kids to see it. Do you think we can go back?"

"This afternoon? Are you sure?" Kevin scratched his head. "I guess we could go after lunch."

At 3:30 we pulled into the village. The weavers were stretched out asleep, but they sat up as we parked next to their awning.

Kevin greeted them with a wide smile and an out-stretched hand. "Asalam alaykum! Kaif halikum? [Peace/Greetings. How are you?]"

The men answered and grinned, motioning for Kevin to join them. Jaden sat down with Kevin. The men showed us the futas they had completed and offered Kevin a twig of qat. They offered Jaden a leaf too, but Kevin declined both with a smile.

I looked down the alley. A woman waved to me from her doorway, stepping out to greet me. She was followed by her neighbors and children, who appeared from multiple doorways. They crowded around Madison, Jack and me with smiling faces and curious eyes.

"*Hadtha koyis* [This is good]." The woman tugged my balto sleeve and touched my hejab.

"Ta'allee, ta'allee [Come, come]," her neighbor beck-oned. Another woman pinched Jack's cheek and kissed him as three older girls encircled Madison, chattering excitedly in Arabic. Madison smiled uncertainly. Jack scowled.

We were led through a concrete home to the back porch. "*Barrood* [Cool]," the woman of the house explained.

We sat on a wooden bench under a thatched awning propped high with skinny tree trunks. The group crowded around, pushing to get a closer look. The woman of the house whispered something to her neighbor, who scuttled into the alley. I heard her call to someone else as she hurried away.

Our hostess looked at me and the children and asked "Mussihiya [Christian]?"

I nodded, looking at the faces gathered around me. "I follow God through the Way, Jesus," I said evenly.

Our hostess went inside her home and returned with a small photograph carefully displayed in an oversized, scratched-up frame. She smiled proudly as she handed it to me. "*Bentee. Ismaha Miriam: Mairr-ee.* [My daughter. Her name is Miriam: Mary]."

She pronounced the word carefully in English. She knew Mary was an important name in Christianity. She seemed proud of her daughter's connection to it.

I tried not to show my surprise. I congratulated her and complimented her daughter's name. I admired the fine photograph and smiled as she pulled her five-year-old daughter from the crowd for me to greet in person. The little girl grinned, reaching out to touch the embroidery on my balto. I pinched her cheek and kissed my fingers, in their custom. Then I introduced my children to the crowd. Madison gave the swarm of women a shaky smile. Jack buried his head as hands reached for his cheeks and curly white hair. I explained that my older son, Jaden, was with his father and the men. The women nodded approvingly.

I asked them about their village and the futas. They took me into the dirt yard to show me vats of dye and colored thread drying on a wire clothesline. A basket of snow-white thread sat waiting beside the vats. I touched the drying colors and complimented their fine work. Their faces beamed as they showed me stacks of futas ready to be washed in the sea.

The neighbor returned from the alley with a tray of cream-filled cookies and a single tin cup, which was filled with water and a floating cube of ice and carefully served to me. I took the cup like a treasure, knowing the effort it had taken to provide it in a village without electricity or running water.

Madison and Jack reached for the cup together. "I'm thirsty." Madison took a big gulp.

Jack took the cup after Madison, and we drank it dry together, thanking the women profusely. I prayed silently for protection against amoebas. We ate the cookies as the women watched. I motioned for them to take some but they declined with wide grins. I praised them for their generosity. The women smiled their pleasure.

Kevin's voice called from the alley. "I must go," I told the women. "My husband is calling me. But, God willing, I will see you another time."

"You must," the women answered in unison. "You must come back and visit us again."

On our car trip home I fingered the futas Kevin had purchased. I thought about the crowd of hands that had waved good-bye to us.

"Feel better?" Kevin reached for my hand.

"I do," I answered. "I may have lost my English-speaking friends, but I feel like I gained an entire village." I sat silent for a minute. "You know, Kevin. It matters how I present myself to them."

After several months in the Tihama, we requested and received permission from the mission board to return to the U.S. for a six-week advocacy trip to speak to churches across the country. We logged nine thousand miles on a borrowed minivan while introducing God's people to the people of the Tihama and calling them to pray and partner with us. Two weeks into our advocacy trip, Kevin and I faced a potential detour. We discovered I was pregnant—at 42.

Four weeks later we returned to the Tihama, and I found myself housebound with constant morning sickness. After losing yet another meal, I washed my face with cool water and returned to my recliner. "Lord, why now?" I cried. "When there's so much to be done, why this pregnancy now?"

I felt caged in when doors were opening all around us. Neighbors of neighbors invited me to visit. Villages invited us to initiate projects. So many things we had prayed for were happening. And I was sidelined to a recliner, fighting to keep food down.

But God's people were praying.

A month later I met my neighbor Firdoos, who not only invited me to visit but also invited our neighbor Nabila to join us. We sat together in the one-room hut that Firdoos shared with her husband, an electrician's apprentice. The cement hut was attached to the outside wall of a two-story villa. Firdoos told me the villa stood empty most of the year. Its owners lived in Sana'a and came to Hudaydah during winter months.

I sat on the thin mattress that served as both mufraj and bed. Firdoos and Nabila fastened curious eyes on me as we drank hot, sweet tea served black with pink sugar wafers. I wondered if Firdoos could afford milk.

I initiated conversation, attempting to understand their lives. "Do you have relatives in Hudaydah?" They did not.

"Do you see your family often?" They went home once a year for *eid al kabeer* [the big festival a month after Ramadhan]. Firdoos went to Taiz, Nabila to her village in the south.

Firdoos was a new bride of eighteen, yet to become pregnant. She had moved to Hudaydah from Taiz, where she had not finished high school. She was slightly plump and looked like she was smiling even when she was not. She wore a thin gold necklace, which she fingered proudly, and a thick black ponytail she displayed uncovered inside her home. She stayed alone while her husband spent long hours each day working or chewing qat with his friends.

Firdoos had a small black and white television that played one channel. The thin maroon curtains in her one open window had been sewn by hand. I could see the uneven line of orange stitches. Firdoos wanted to learn how to sew dresses. She dreamed of being a seamstress.

Her one tiny bathroom had a hole in the cement floor and a bucket of water next to the hole. There was no running water and no kitchen. Her water came from a faucet outside her back door. Her two-burner hot plate was perched on a concrete block next to the faucet.

Nabila lived in an open shack in the yard of the villa across the street. I had seen the shack from my window. I had thought the rough lean-to was an animal pen. I had seen an oil lantern on a peg at night, but it had been beyond me to imagine the lean-to as someone's home. My heart lurched when I learned that Nabila shared it with her husband, a tire repairman, and their three-year-old son, Mohammed. It lurched even more when I learned that the undersized, barrel-chested little boy sitting next to Nabila was her third child. Her first two had died from malaria and unknown causes.

Nabila was thin but full-bosomed with a face too old for her nineteen years. She had not gone to school. In her village only boys were educated. Her brown eyes looked dismal even when she laughed. She sighed when she mentioned her dead children. She did not seem mournful; she seemed resigned.

"*Kan al qadar* [It was their fate]," she said, moving her shoulders in a tired shrug.

I looked at the tiny boy beside her. Mohammed's brown curls crowned large brown eyes that drank everything in, including me. He stared intently at me. My attempts to make him laugh failed. I wondered if he ever laughed. His chest was puffed out like a strutting rooster. At first I thought it was intentional, that the undersized child was trying to look bigger. But I soon realized he was not. I wondered if his mother knew the signs of malnutrition and parasites.

His mother's head scarf slipped from her head to her shoulder as we talked, exposing her greased brown hair. She did not seem to notice, but Mohammed seemed almost alarmed. He quickly moved the scarf back in place and smoothed it gently back over her hair. He tenderly patted her covered head.

"Shukran, habibi [Thank you, my love]." Nabila kissed him.

Our visit ended after an hour and a half. Firdoos's husband roared up on his motorcycle, and I knew it was time to leave. I invited Firdoos and Nabila to visit me. They nodded with pleased smiles, but their wary eyes told me they would not come. They urged me to return the next day with my children.

"B'ahowel [I will try]," I replied as I went out the door.

Nabila walked to her lean-to as I walked across the dusty alley to my home, a house that was more like a villa than a hut. I had been proud of our new house and its comforts. We had been led to it by local businessmen who insisted it was the house we should have. But now I was not sure.

I thought about Firdoos and Nabila, barely out of their girlhood. I thought about the challenges common to their everyday lives. They seemed resigned to things I would not tolerate. I was beginning to understand their curiosity. They were less curious about me than they were about why I wanted to know them. Those who lived in villas never spoke to those who lived in huts. Villa-dwellers pretended that no one else was there.

I unlocked my gate, muttering to myself. "How easy it is to let lives go unnoticed. Lord, keep me from letting any life slip by." I went into my house and shut the door behind me.

12

We pulled off the asphalt highway and bounced along a narrow dirt road. "Ouch! Can you imagine this in monsoon season? Look at the potholes!" I rubbed my head where it had hit the car window and braced the small bulge in my abdomen.

"Sorry." Kevin looked over his shoulder at me on the backseat. "I didn't see that one. You okay?" he steered sideways to avoid another hole in the road.

The guide in the front passenger seat grabbed his armrest. Kevin grinned at Omar. "Praise God for four-wheel drives!"

"You doing okay, Annie?" I looked at the young nurse beside me. "A little different from Virginia, huh?"

Annie laughed, reaching for the camera that had bounced off the seat. "Yeah, but I'm glad you let me come along. This will be the highlight of my trip."

"Glad you could come. I needed a partner. I don't know any Christians who have been to this village yet. It's pretty remote. You'll have lots to tell your church."

"That's a fact!" Annie grinned.

I grinned back, but my smile slowly faded as I recalled my retort to Omar. Omar's arrogance about his pure connection to Abraham and his disparaging remarks about the Bible and Jesus had spurred me to hot anger. It was my Lord he was making a common prophet and my Bible he was deriding as corrupt.

I chewed my lip. I had nailed him with the differences between Jesus' life and Mohammed's, and I had won the debate. Omar would not venture another remark about Jesus or the Bible to me. But winning the argument had cost me an opportunity to demonstrate the loving relationship God offered to all people through the only way they could have it—through Jesus, His Messiah.

I peered out of the window, letting my head bump hard against the glass. *Oh, Lord,* I cried inwardly. *How can You use me when my mouth keeps getting in the way?*

I looked far beyond the dusty, difficult road to the endless expanse of clear, blue sky. *Lord, I need to focus on You, to worship You in all I do, in front of everyone I meet. If I am doing that, then everything else will fall into place.*

The dirt road sliced the middle of a field edged by acacia bushes and a few banana trees. Dried grass waved gently on both sides as the road cut deeper through the field. A lone donkey grazed near the roadside, and a skinny brown cow grazed just beyond. They were undisturbed by our SUV, but a long-legged crane flapped its white wings and flew away as we passed.

This was our first invitation into one of hundreds of Tihama villages. We had received invitations almost overnight. Doors that had not even been cracked now appeared wide open. We thanked God for the faithful prayers of His people and prayed for more workers as we struggled to be in several places at the same time.

We pulled up on a sandy knoll under a large shade tree, and Kevin turned off the car engine. "We're here!"

"Al hamdulilah." Omar stretched as he got out of the car.

I looked at the village. A six-foot, mud-plastered wall surrounded a collection of ten or eleven huts. I could see only their round thatched roofs. A slight breeze rustled as a dove cooed in the thatch. A goat bleated in the distance.

"Ahlen wa sahlen! [Hello and welcome!]" The young sheikh walked out of an opening in the wall. Two men accompanied him with wide smiles and curious eyes. They greeted Kevin, and he walked side by side into the village with them. Annie and I followed behind.

Inside the wall, surprisingly large brown mud huts were scattered about sandy soil. Each had two square openings that served as windows and a single door propped open at the center. They were made of mud bricks plastered and painted with different shades of brown. Their roofs were thatched with bamboo reeds, branches and woven bark from palm trees.

A woman appeared in the door of one of the larger huts. She hurried to greet me, introducing herself as the sheikh's sister, and hugged me enthusiastically as I kissed her cheeks and greeted her. I introduced Annie, and we walked hand-in-hand with her toward her hut.

A baby was crying nearby. I looked around, trying to locate the sound. Lying in the dirt three feet away was a naked baby girl not more than six or seven months old. She flayed her arms and legs and wailed pitifully as she wriggled on the ground. I flinched, moving involuntarily toward her.

The sheikh's sister stopped me. "*Ahdee,* ahdee [It's okay, it's okay]." She nudged me toward the hut.

"But the baby? Why is she in the dirt?" I paused.

"Ahdee, ahdee," she repeated. "The baby soiled her clothes. It is nothing."

She introduced me to the other five women in the hut and motioned us to the center cot, one of four circling the inside wall. "Glissee, glissee [Sit, sit]."

The cots were wooden with rope rungs and thin foam pads strewn with flowered cushions. Our hostess grabbed three or four and plumped them against the wall. She waved us to make ourselves comfortable.

"Why is that baby in the dirt?" Annie whispered as we sat on the cot. "Doesn't she know how dangerous that is?"

"They don't even know how dangerous unboiled water is," I whispered back. "That's why we need nurses like you for health education!"

"Somebody needs to get that baby." Annie was angry.

"She said the baby soiled her clothes, but it's more than that. I've never seen a baby treated that way. Look, someone got her."

We watched a woman pass by with the baby. She was scolding the crying infant, holding her under her arm like a sack of potatoes.

I shook my head. "Something's up with that. They don't usually treat babies that way."

The women seated themselves on the cots around us and stared curiously. A few young girls sat between them, smiling shyly as they leaned on each other's arms. A teenage girl had been reciting something from a torn piece of paper to an older woman. She stared at us along with the rest of the group.

Several flies buzzed in through the open door. I cleared my throat and commented on the beauty of the village and the sweet quiet far from the highway. I told them how refreshing it was to hear the breeze in the grass instead of car horns and motorcycles.

They smiled their pleasure and began to relax. They asked about my children, wondering why I had not brought them. I explained that they were doing their schoolwork at home with my friend. I did not mention my hesitation to take them to a remote village without exploring it first.

The teenager began reciting lines again from her torn piece of paper. The older woman, who looked about sixty, repeated each line after the girl. I listened to the somber recitation. The girl was helping the woman memorize a *surah* [chapter] from the Quran. The older woman, who turned out to be 45, did not know how to read.

"She goes to school," my hostess said proudly, pointing to the teenager. "She is the daughter of my sister from the town."

I smiled at the girl, who sat straighter and read more carefully from her scrap of paper. "Is there a school in your village?" I asked the other women.

"For boys only. In the town there is a school where girls can study."

"What are they saying?" Annie whispered. I quickly translated the women's words.

Annie looked shocked. "There's no school for the girls? How do they learn to read and write?"

"They don't. Tihama villages have an illiteracy rate of 98 percent among women. What they know, they learn from memorization or by word of mouth. They can't read it for themselves, not even their religion. They know it only by what they are told it is."

Tears glistened in Annie's eyes. "Somebody needs to tell them God's Word," she whispered.

"I know." I held her eyes. "They need to hear it for themselves."

One of the women rummaged underneath her cot and pulled out a small stereo cassette player. She checked the batteries and put in a cassette. She motioned a woman to join her as Arabic music crooned from the player.

"Do you dance?" the woman asked me.

"Akeed [Of course]." I grinned. "Yemeni dances are beautiful."

Pleased, the woman wrapped a scarf around her hips and began to sashay with a partner. "Get ready," I whispered to Annie. "Our turn will come."

"I can't dance like that," Annie protested.

"Just shake everything that's shakable. No one will care if you mess up."

Annie looked skeptical but stepped obligingly at her turn. We danced until the batteries slowed the music to a deviant drone. Then we sat on our cots and passed around bottles of lukewarm water.

The women began to ask about our families in America and how we liked living in Yemen. Our answers were interrupted by our hostess.

"You have a camera!" she exclaimed, eyeing my camera bag. "Would you make pictures of my children?"

The other women agreed eagerly. "Aywa, aywa [Yes, yes]!" All eyes were on me.

"Akeed [Of course]." I loaded more film as the women scurried for their children, who were playing with goats in the animal pen.

After twenty minutes, one woman hurried breathlessly back with her daughter. The little girl was dressed in a purple satin dress with tulle flounces around the hem. Her hair was slicked into a tight bun, and her cheeks were damp and shiny. Other women joined us soon after with their children dressed in their best clothes. I was surprised to see the baby girl we had seen in the dirt. She was cleaned and dressed in a pink ruffled dress made of satin.

"That's the baby," I whispered to Annie.

I looked at our hostess. "Whose daughter is this?" I asked.

The women looked uncertainly at each other. My hostess, Arwa, laughed nervously. "Her mother is not here," she said and looked at me warily.

"The pictures will be better outside," I said.

Each of the mothers took turns arranging their children. They cajoled the children for each shot, moving themselves a safe distance from my camera lens. The children were too intent on me to listen to their mothers. They stared at my protruding lens as if it were a weapon. At their mothers' coaxing, a few smiled nervously, but a few seemed ready to cry. I snapped pictures quickly, distributing candy from my pockets as I finished each shot.

When they were finished, the children scampered off to play, and the women went inside the hut. I packed away my camera, explaining to Annie that conservative Muslim mothers would not allow pictures in their homes because they considered them to be forbidden graven images.

"But many make exceptions for their children's pictures," I said. "Even if they won't let themselves be photographed."

"Are they afraid of the camera? Like it will steal their soul or something?"

I laughed. "No. They are afraid their picture might be viewed by men in the film development process."

I suddenly became aware of a man watching us. He was tall and looked a little like the sheikh. I started to nod a greeting to him, but I realized he was not looking at us. He seemed to be looking through us. His eyes were far off, staring blankly as he muttered something and walked around in circles. His hand passed methodically over his face as he walked.

"That must be the sheikh's brother," I whispered. "We were told he had a mentally disabled brother."

"Ta'allee [Come]," Arwa called to us from the doorway. She clicked her tongue when she saw the man walking in circles. "*Muskeen* [Pitiful]," she said softly. She waved him gently toward another hut.

"Does he live in that house?" I asked.

"Aywa. He lives with my mother. His wife is . . . she is not here."

"He is married?" I tried to keep the surprise from my voice.

"Akeed. He is the brother of a sheikh. But he is *taban* [tired, sick]."

"What did she say?" Annie urged me to translate.

"She was telling me about that man. He is married to a woman who is not here. The way she said it makes me think something must have happened. The wife must have run off."

"Do you think she was forced to marry him?" Annie grimaced. "I can't say I'd blame her for running off."

"Maybe. A sheikh would have a lot of influence. Hey!" I looked at her. "I wonder if she was the mother of that baby girl."

"Is that why that baby is treated so badly? Because the mother ran off?"

"Maybe. Or the mother was raped and unmarried." I looked thoughtfully at her, then glanced at Arwa who was scowling at us. We entered the hut quickly and sat on the cot, tucking our feet under our skirts to keep from showing their bottoms.

I caught a whiff of a wood fire. "Is something burning?" I asked Arwa.

"They are cooking the bread for lunch," Arwa explained. "Come, I will show you."

We followed as she led us outside to a round cement pit in the ground. It was three feet in diameter and less than three feet deep. Wood and charcoal burned in the bottom, heating the sides to a fiery hot. A woman took balls of dough and flattened them, twirling them in her hands like miniature pizzas. She handed them to another woman, who slapped them inside the oven pit. After they had baked, the woman scooped them out with a stick and stacked them in a straw basket.

The bread smelled wonderful. "I'm starving," I whispered to Annie. The women smiled, understanding my meaning. "Besurah [Quickly]," Arwa said.

Back inside the hut, the baby girl swung in a hammock made from a strip of cloth tied between two cots. She had been given a bottle of milk to drink by herself as the women sat around chatting. Suddenly one of the women shrieked and clicked her tongue. I followed her eyes. A thin trickle dripped from the hammock to puddle on the dirt floor.

The woman marched to the hammock and jerked the baby out. She scolded her, stripping the soiled pink satin from the baby's startled body. The baby began to cry. The woman thrust her outward with her arms and marched outside.

"Don't they use diapers?" Annie objected.

"No. Most women can't afford them. How would they get them out here anyway?"

I strained to see the woman, who returned a few minutes later without the baby. I could hear her crying in the distance. She had been placed in the dirt somewhere beyond our hut. Tears sprang to my eyes as Annie and I both wriggled uncomfortably on our cot. I looked at Arwa, who was watching me with eyes full of warning.

I struggled with my emotions. "I want to take that baby in my arms and show her what love is," I whispered angrily.

"Can't we do something?" Annie echoed my feelings.

I looked at Arwa, who continued to watch me steadily. I swallowed and gripped the sides of the cot. "No," I said finally, my eyes still on Arwa's. "It could cost us every relationship in this village and get us nowhere with the baby either. Adoption by Christians is not permitted."

Annie and I settled uncomfortably against the cushions. I tried to keep my ears from straining toward the baby's cries. My heart felt torn between saving one baby and saving an entire village.

I sighed and smiled at Arwa. She nodded, content with my response. She stood and motioned for the other women. It was time for their prayers. The women went out of the hut to wash their faces, arms and lower legs as required by Islamic law.

"Annie, are you up to praying with me after the women finish their prayers?"

"In Arabic?" Her eyes were panicked.

"No," I laughed. "In English. Just follow my lead."

The women returned and rolled out their prayer mats, lining them side by side along the dirt floor of the hut. They stood next to each other on the rugs and then knelt to begin their prayers. They recited them quickly in unison, performing their prostrations together. When they finished, they began to re-roll the rugs to slide under a cot.

I stood, pulling Annie up with me. "My friend and I would like to pray." I said.

Arwa looked incredulous. "You pray?" she gasped.

I smiled. "Of course, I pray. Many times, every day."

She struggled with my words. She was perplexed by them. "She can't believe we pray," I explained softly to Annie.

"Why?" Annie was as perplexed as Arwa.

"Because all she's ever heard about Christian women is that we are immoral, corrupt people who cheat on our husbands and don't love our children. We're probably the first Christians she has ever actually met."

Arwa's eyes were wide with curiosity as she motioned a woman to put the rugs back in place. All of the women stared at us, watching to see what we would do. I took a deep breath and stepped toward the prayer rug, taking Annie's hand.

"Don't you wash?" Arwa stopped me. Her voice rang sharply, like an accusation.

I looked evenly at her. "Our Book teaches that to be clean on the outside is not enough. To come into the presence of God, we must be clean on the inside. Man looks at what is on the outside, but God looks at what is inside of us. He requires our hearts to be clean. That's why Jesus came, to make us clean in our hearts."

All eyes were on me, appraising my every move. Arwa looked intently and finally nodded. "What you say is good," she said.

She moved aside to let Annie and me kneel on the rugs. Then she and the women stepped back to watch.

Annie and I joined hands. We knelt together on the rugs and bowed our heads. We prayed one after the other aloud in English. We asked God to open the women's hearts to know Him and to understand the truth about Jesus. We prayed that they would recognize their need to be internally clean, and we asked God to bring His Word to them in a way they could understand. We finished our prayers and stood from the rugs.

Arwa crossed her arms across her chest. "Your prayers are short," she chided me. Their prayers had been long recitations, interjected with many prostrations.

I settled back against my cushions. "When we pray, Arwa, we don't recite prayers," I said. "We talk to God personally from our hearts, because we pray in Jesus' name. Sometimes I pray for a long time, talking to God about many things. But sometimes my prayers are shorter, to thank Him for something or to praise Him. My prayers are not the same every time."

The women stared at me as if I were from another planet. This was something they had never heard before. I was not what these women had expected. I did not seem to fit their image of who Christian women were supposed to be.

Two women walked in with trays of food. Arwa helped the others take large straw mats from a hook on the wall and lay them on the dirt floor. The women set down trays of rice with stewed mutton and vegetables. My stomach grumbled, even at the bowl of slimy *melokhia*, a dish that tasted like spinach but looked like stewed weeds. It made most foreigners as green as it was, but we were ravenous.

Annie and I bowed our heads and thanked God for the meal as the women watched. Then along with the women we dived into the food. Our eagerness pleased the women. We dipped our hands into the food with theirs, tearing pieces of bread shared between us. We ate as they had eaten for hundreds of years.

I enjoyed every bite, even though I knew that as women, we were eating the leftovers from the men's meal. They had been served at 1:30. I glanced at my watch. We were eating well past 3:00.

After our meal, we lay back against our cushions. I was full and sleepy, content to chat lazily with the women, who also seemed pleasantly relaxed.

"Audra!" I could hear Kevin's voice calling from the opening to the village.

I turned my head slowly as a boy ran into our hut. "Your husband is calling you!" he panted.

I sighed and looked regretfully at the women. "I must go. My husband is calling me." Annie and I gathered our baltos and hejabs.

Arwa shook her head. "No, not yet. Stay longer, please. Your husband can stay with the men. It is early. Please. Glissee."

I smiled apologetically. "I must go home to my children. It is a long drive still to Hudaydah, and I must get home to give them their dinner."

Arwa pleaded with me to stay. She was joined by the others who begged us to stay for the night, or even the week.

"Send for your children. Your friend can bring them," a woman urged.

I was touched by their insistence. It seemed urgent, as if they were afraid we would not come back.

"I will return," I smiled, "and I will bring my children. Next time maybe we can stay for more than one day."

"You must," Arwa whispered as she hugged me. "You must come back and visit us next week! Thursday and Friday!"

I hugged each of the women in turn, kissing their cheeks and thanking them for the lovely day. Annie did the same. We turned to wave to the women as they stood crowding the doorway of their hut.

"Ma'a salama [Good-bye]," I called.

"Ma'a salama," they called back, watching me walk away from them and out of their village. I swallowed a lump in my throat as I joined Kevin.

"Did you women have a good time?" Kevin asked as he and Omar climbed into the front and buckled their seat belts.

"A lovely time. How about you?" I stowed my camera bag beneath my seat.

"It was good. Lots of opportunities." Kevin caught my eye, and I nodded.

We pulled away from the village, bumping back along the dirt road. My heart felt as heavy as the sun sinking into the horizon. I turned to look back at the village, almost wanting to go back. But it was only one village, and there were many more like it.

I looked at Annie, who was already asleep against the window. I sighed. *Lord, Kevin and I can't do this without more help. Send more workers,* I pleaded. *The harvest is ripe. Send workers into the harvest fields.*

We pulled onto the asphalt highway, leaving the bumpy village road behind us. I settled into my seat as the last rays of sunlight flickered away. In the distance I saw another village. It was similar to the one we had left, a cluster of mud huts with thatched roofs and a single well in the middle. It was just another village without electricity and running water. But my eyes were caught by what was next to it: huge power lines carrying electricity from the energy plant in the south to the cities in the north.

I stared at it. The village had the source of light all around it, but the village remained in darkness. It was if it did not even know the source was there.

The words of John 1 rang in my ears: "In Him was life, and the life was the light of men. And the light shines in the darkness, and the darkness did not comprehend it" (John 1:4–5, NKJV).

Tears streamed silently down my face as I watched the village pass. I saw another one not far beyond it. I thought of the women we had just left. There were millions in the Tihama just like them.

Oh, Lord, I cried. *Bring the message of Your Light into the darkness in a way the people can understand. Send workers to help connect the people to You.*

13

I walked down the long stretch of gray sand, watching the sun glitter on dancing waves. Seagulls twittered overhead as small crabs scurried from my path. Madison and Jack scampered about, brandishing blue buckets as they searched for hermit crabs. Jaden and Kevin splashed behind us in the gray-green sea. I smiled, glad to be on the remote strip of sand thirty kilometers from the city. It was a place where we were undisturbed by prying eyes. I felt the sweetness of life around me and within me as I approached the end of my second trimester.

An organization at home had committed to send a team to work with us for a short-term project. They had prayed for us and partnered with us spiritually. Now they would partner with us physically, joining us side by side. I was eager for their arrival. The task ahead of us was huge. We could not meet it without the involvement of God's people.

A large gray mass bulged on the sand ahead of me. I approached it, wary and watchful, cautiously inching closer. It was a giant sea turtle, weighing about three hundred pounds. Lying on its back on a crest of sand, beyond the reach of the ocean, its thick tail was slashed deep; the bloody wound gaped open. Its eyes were closed, and its huge head hung limply down.

I sighed to myself. "I guess endangered species aren't a big deal in Yemen."

I turned quickly around and headed back toward the children. "Madison! Jaden! Come here!" I called. "I want to show you something!"

The children dropped their buckets and ran to me. "See what, Mommy? What do you want to show us?" Madison asked. I led them to the gigantic turtle.

"Poor turtle! Can't we do something to help him?" Madison's lip trembled.

"I think it's too late, honey," I said softly. "He looks beyond hope."

"How did he get upside down?" Jaden ran up to join us.

"Probably from the fishermen," I answered. "They wanted fish, not turtles. He must have gotten caught in their net and they cut him out. See his tail?"

Madison nodded. "But why did they just leave him to die?" The tremor in her voice grew.

"Sweetheart, the fishermen were trying to make a living. The turtle got in their way and probably tore their net. Maybe they were mad. They need their net to make money."

Jaden clapped sand from his hands. "They could have rolled him over on his tummy. Then he could have crawled back into the sea and lived."

Jaden bent to peer under the shell to examine the turtle's head. Suddenly, without warning, the head moved. Jaden shot in the air backward, landing close beside me. Madison and Jack both jumped back with him, startled and uncertain. I pulled them close, alarmed myself. We stared together at the turtle, which was not dead. He opened his eyes and began to open and close his mouth.

I burst out laughing. "Jaden, I've never seen you move so fast in your life! You were airborne!"

Jaden grinned sheepishly. "I thought he was dead."

"So did I! He looked like it, didn't he?"

The turtle let his head fall back to the sand after another attempt to open his mouth. I stopped chuckling.

"I don't know if he wants to bite us or if he just needs water," I said. "He's been lying in the sun since early morning. Madison, go get your bucket," I directed. "Jaden, Jack—let's pour water on him and see if it helps. We need to flip him over."

I shoved my weight against the turtle, grunting. "I . . . can't . . . budge him. Help me, Jaden."

Jaden leaned in to help, and Jack added his small frame to Jaden's. The three of us shoved together but were not successful. "We need more help." I stood back and wiped my face. I was breathing heavily.

"Jaden, go get Daddy. Maybe he can help us flip him over."

"I'm here." Kevin ran up with Madison, each carrying plastic buckets. "Let's all get on one side and push together."

"Watch out for his mouth," I warned.

We almost could not do it. Our strength was no match for the turtle's weight. But on our fifth attempt, with everyone pushing together, we flipped him to his belly. The turtle raised his head, but he was too weak to move.

"Everybody get water!" I yelled. "Let's pour it on him!"

We poured bucket after bucket of seawater and watched as the turtle raised his head. The water seemed to revive him. He opened and closed his mouth repeatedly, turning his head for more.

"He's saying thank you," Jack said. We laughed.

"We need to get him into the ocean," I said. "He might have a chance to survive."

"What are we going to name him?" Madison asked.

"Hmmm . . . how about Herbert?" I poured another bucket of water. "Herbert, the giant sea turtle."

"Here, Herbert. Drink some water." Jack poured a bucket over his head. Herbert's mouth gaped toward Jack.

Our buckets were small and our water meager compared to what the turtle needed. I looked out at the vast ocean, so close and yet beyond Herbert's reach.

"Let's see if we can move him closer to the water. If we can get him to the surf, then we might be able to slide him in." Kevin tried to heave him forward. Herbert would not budge.

"Let's all try!" I pushed alongside Kevin, joined by the children. We pushed together, but nothing happened. We heaved again, but we could not move him. We were no match for the giant turtle. We needed more people.

Kevin wiped his forehead and looked toward the ocean. "Maybe the tide will be high enough to pull him out to sea."

I looked at Herbert. He was right on the shoreline, his body lying halfway over the high tide mark and halfway beyond it. If Herbert survived until the tide reached him, he would still need help moving into the sea.

I looked at three small pairs of anxious eyes. "That could work," I offered hopefully. "If we can give him enough water, he might live until the tide reaches him."

"The sun is going down, Audra," Kevin whispered. "We need to leave soon."

"Just a little while longer," I pleaded. "We might be able to save him. He is an endangered species, you know."

"Everything is an endangered species in Yemen," Kevin said wryly.

Herbert lifted his head for each one of our water buckets. We tried once more to push Herbert into the sea, but we were not successful.

The last sliver of orange sun dipped into the horizon, and the sky began to grow dark. Kevin motioned for us to leave.

"One more bucket. Please, Daddy!" Madison pleaded.

Kevin sighed, looking at his watch. "All right. One more. Everybody get one more bucket to pour on Herbert."

We poured our last buckets, sloshing as much water as we could into Herbert's gaping mouth. Madison patted the top of his speckled shell. "Good-bye, Herbert," she said. "The tide is coming to take you back to the ocean."

I pulled her gently away. "We need to go, honey. We've done our best. Look how much better Herbert is than when we first found him."

Madison nodded. "But is it enough to save him, Mommy?"

I sighed. "I hope so, honey. We've done all we can."

Madison was ready to cry. Kevin took her hand and gently started walking. "We have to go, honey. We should have left an hour ago. If it gets too dark, we won't be able to find the path back to the highway."

"Yes, it's time." I pulled Jaden and Jack away.

We walked into our house an hour later to the sound of the telephone ringing. I set down the pot of hot stewed beans and khobz [flatbread] from the corner mata'am [restaurant] and answered the phone. Kevin hauled towels and beach toys from the car.

"Mrs. Shelby?"

"Yes?"

"Ma'am, this is Sergeant Medlin from the United States Embassy in Sana'a calling to inform you that a U.S. military ship was bombed in Aden this morning by Islamic terrorists. We are advising all American citizens to avoid public places and maintain vigilance at all times, exercising extreme caution and observing travel warnings as posted by the U.S. State Department. Our records show you have five in your family in Hudaydah. Is this correct?"

I swallowed. "Yes."

"Ma'am, we urge you to exercise extreme caution, maintain contact with your business office in Sana'a and devise your course of action according to the State Department's recommendations."

"Was anyone hurt?" I asked. My knees felt weak.

"Yes, ma'am. Several military personnel were killed. We are waiting to confirm casualty reports. Ma'am, do you have any questions or need any assistance?"

"No. Thank you, Sergeant, for calling."

I hung up the phone and looked at Kevin, who was waiting impatiently beside me. I repeated the sergeant's words, struggling with the lump in my throat.

"Oh, wow," Kevin sighed. "This will make news. We need to let our families know that we're okay. They've probably already heard about it."

"Yeah. Let's eat supper and get the kids down. Then we can start sending e-mails." I sighed deeply. "Life in Yemen."

A week later I yelled at Kevin from my computer. "I can't believe it! They cancelled their mission trip! Aden is seven hours from here! It did not even affect us!"

"I know, but they are trying to exercise good judgment." Kevin looked like I felt, as if the wind had stopped blowing and our sails were hanging limp and useless.

"I just can't believe it!"

"There are travel warnings against coming here, you know." Kevin leaned back in his chair and looked out of the window.

"When have there not been warnings? They knew there were risks when they made the commitment."

"I guess the risks became real with the Aden bombing."

"How are we going to tell people that the help we promised is cancelled? We can't do this work alone, Kevin! It's too huge! We needed them!" I threw my address book across the window and burst into tears. I dabbed them brusquely with a tissue.

I buried my head in my hands and let my tears flow. "I feel betrayed, Kevin. They promised to partner with us. But they won't face what we face."

"Audra, they're not going to willingly put their team in danger."

"I know that with my head, Kevin. I understand! But not with my heart." I wiped my eyes with a tissue.

I thought of the photograph released of the two terrorists in their little wooden boat. About to hit the side of the U.S.S. *Cole*, one of the young men had stood and saluted, confident that his suicide assured him entrance into paradise. I held my head and wept again to think of his deception.

I took a deep breath and blew my nose before shutting down my computer. "We'll have to figure something out or these opportunities will slip away. More people will die without the Truth. We can't do this without more help."

I sighed deeply and looked out of the window at the dark sky. I thought back to the afternoon, remembering the children's laughter as they raced down the sand to find Herbert. I saw again their hurt when they found his bones scattered in the place where he had been.

"I'm going to check on the kids."

"Aren't they asleep?" Kevin looked puzzled. "They should sleep hard after playing at the beach today."

"I'd feel better if I checked on them." I sighed. "They were pretty upset when we found Herbert's bones."

"Yeah, they were," Kevin agreed. "That was pretty sad. So close to the water, but he could not make it in."

We would not allow ourselves to feel defeated. For the next two months we pressed on, entering doors that opened before us. But we were stretched thin. My advancing pregnancy had brought complications, and I would need to return to the U.S. for delivery. I limited my afternoon visits, keeping them within Hudaydah. I was introduced to a family who welcomed me with constant invitations. I was delighted to meet the married daughters of this multi-family home, although Amal and her sisters soon became possessive of my time.

One afternoon I sat in Amal's long concrete block room watching the breeze blow through the entrance. Qat leaves and dirt stirred on the cement floor as the breeze teased plastic bags of clothing in a corner. A rusty fan groaned in circles overhead. Thin padded cots lined three sides of the room, where a stray black shoe peeked from the dust underneath.

The women visiting on my left were intent on their advice to fifteen-year-old Hadil, Almal's eldest daughter. A prospective groom had begun negotiations to marry her.

"You must seek a full wedding set—a necklace, earrings and bracelet. Maybe two rings also." The woman stretched her plump arm to jingle her gold bracelets in front of the girl. Several rings flashed on her chubby fingers. "The groom must give much gold for you."

"Yes, yes," agreed the woman next to her as she took a long draw on the water pipe. "See how her husband values her?" She nodded appreciatively at the plump woman. "You are a pretty girl, Hadil. Your father is known in your village. You will get much gold." She passed the water pipe to a thin woman in a fraying dera.

The thin woman wore no jewelry. Her face was worn and wrinkled, but not by time. Her hard, weathered hands raised the pipe to a thin mouth filled with brown teeth.

"The gold will provide for you," she agreed softly. "It is important for your children."

The future bride looked down at her hands, blushing at the mention of children. "Ensha'allah," Hadil whispered shyly.

I watched Hadil, but I was thinking of other prospective brides I had seen with their mothers. After a bride's price was decided with the groom, mothers took their daughters into gold shops to haggle with shopkeepers, pursuing the most gold they could buy with the money. I shifted on my cot. I had also seen women bargain in the shops to sell back their wedding gold while big-eyed children clung to their skirts. Those women were not brides or widows; they were the mothers of hungry children, married to qat-chewing men.

Hadil's eyes flashed with excitement as her mother, Amal, described her prospective groom. "He is a good boy, the son of my husband's sister. He works in a shoe factory in Taiz. He will be a good husband to Hadil."

Hadil smiled, looking through the open doorway, past the warped tin fence of her father's compound. I saw dreams in her eyes. I imagined her sitting in her white gown on her decorated throne in the center of the women's celebration. My eyes caught those of Nasimah, who sat next to Hadil. Nasimah was one of Hadil's girlhood friends, a bride married less than a year. Gold necklaces gleamed below her heavily made-up face. Earrings sparkled at her ears, but there was no sparkle in her eyes, and her red-painted mouth did not smile. She listened wordlessly to the advice, offering no suggestions. She had no dreams in her eyes.

I leaned back against the faded cushions and munched popcorn from my saucer. The last rays of afternoon sun filtered through the high, open windows. The tin roof crackled overhead as it cooled from the daytime heat. A rat scuttled across a ledge behind the women, who ignored it.

Hadil brought in a tray and proudly offered the cake she had baked. It was a yellow cake swirled with chocolate. I wondered where she had baked it. Her mother cooked on a two-burner gas cooktop in the yard and baked her bread in a fire pit made from cement.

Hadil seemed to know my thoughts. "I baked it at my friend's house. She has an oven and a blender, like you make bis bas [salsa]," she explained.

A graying old woman with a lined face and missing teeth leaned forward. "You should use the *motkhenna* for bis bas. It is the best way." She turned to scrutinize me. "You have a motkhenna, yes?" she asked. "Every bride must have a motkhenna for her kitchen."

I tried to understand what she was talking about. "What is a motkhenna?" I asked.

The old woman's eyes widened with surprise. "You do not have a motkhenna? Bring it and show her," the woman commanded Hadil. "Maybe she calls it by another name."

Hadil motioned for Nasimah to help her. They returned lugging a heavy, rectangular stone slab and a stone rolling pin.

"This is a motkhenna," the old woman said triumphantly. "It is important in the kitchen. You can grind wheat or corn for cakes and bread. And you can grind vegetables and tomatoes for sauces. It is daruri [essential] for every wife's kitchen. You must get one from the suq!" She clicked her tongue at me in disapproval.

I smiled. "Yes, I must get one. Thank you for showing me."

The old woman sat back against her cushions with a pleased smile wrinkling her face. She seemed glad to give instruction to a foreign woman. I chuckled inwardly. How could I describe my high-powered food processor to a woman who thought me ill-equipped without a stone grinding slab? I smiled. I would indeed buy a motkhenna, but not for my kitchen. I would display it in my curio cabinet.

"When are you leaving for Amrika?" Amal asked, taking my hand possessively. "I will miss you."

A second rat scuttled along the upper ridge of the wall.

"I will miss you, too," I answered, squeezing her hand. "I will leave after one week. But I will be back after three months. It will not be long. You must come and visit me!"

"Oh, no!" Amal's eyes grew wide. "I am afraid of Amrika. They will rob me on the street or shoot me there!" Her voice trailed to a whisper. "They will rape me."

"No, Amal!" I was shocked. "Why would you think this?"

"My friend tells me. She watches the news from Amrika on the television. Every day there are killings and robberies and raping of women!"

I stared at her in amazement. "It is true there are bad things that happen, Amal. But those things are few. There are many good things, too. The news does not give the truth of what life is like in Amrika."

I paused and cleared my throat. "Amal, do you know that my friends are afraid to come to Yemen?"

She was astonished. "But why?" she asked.

"They are afraid they will be killed by terrorists."

"Oh! But we are not like that, Audra. Only a few!" she exclaimed.

I smiled. "Aywa [Yes]. And Amrika is not like all the bad news you hear. Only a few."

"Ah." Amal nodded. "*Fahamt* [Understood]."

"The doctors are good in Amrika?" she asked cautiously. Her eyes went to her newborn son, asleep in the cloth hammock tied between rusting legs of a cot. He had been injured during delivery, his hip permanently crippled.

The old woman leaned forward. "Your doctor is a man or a woman?" she asked sharply. She waited for my answer. All of the women leaned forward with her to hear.

I struggled, not wanting to lie but unable to admit that my obstetrician was a man. I remembered Fatima's respiratory infection. Her husband had refused to let a male doctor use a stethoscope, even on top of her balto. I looked around at the women. They were afraid of hospitals, terrified of being touched by a male physician. Their babies had been delivered at home.

"There are many good women doctors in America," I said slowly.

The women relaxed against their cushions. The old woman nodded approvingly. "Daruri [Essential]," she said.

"There is a good woman doctor in Sana'a," Amal ventured. "Your baby could be born in Yemen."

I smiled apologetically. "I must return to America, Amal. I have much sickness with this pregnancy. Diabetes. A kidney infection. My blood pressure is high. See how big my legs are?" I lifted the skirts of my dera. "I must go home to my family for the birth. But I will return, and my baby will grow up in Yemen."

The women were delighted. "Ensha'allah," echoed around the room as they clapped. Amal squeezed my hand in hers. "You will have a strong son, ma'a sha'allah," she said.

"Oh no—I want a girl!" I exclaimed. "I have one daughter and two sons. I want my daughter to have a sister."

"No, no! Girls are not good. For them there are many problems!" the women chorused. "Ensha'allah you will have many sons. You are young!"

I laughed. "Four children are enough. I am too old for more!"

Amal looked shocked. "No, Audra," she scolded. "You are not old. Women have babies here until they are fifty, even older!"

I looked at Amal, whom I guessed to be my age. Amal had six children living. She had lost one to malaria, and now her newborn appeared sickly. "Will you have more children?" I asked.

"Ensha'allah [God willing]! More sons!" she declared firmly. Then she sighed and whispered, "But not many more. I am tired."

Jack burst through the doorway, startling us. His face was streaked with dirt. "I'm thirsty," he announced.

Amal took the communal cup from a huge plastic jug and poured water into it. Jack drank it and asked for more.

"What have you been doing?" I asked, trying to wipe some of the grime off his face.

"Breaking soda bottles." He gulped his third cup of water.

"Breaking bottles? Where?" I tried to keep my voice low.

"In the street against the wall. If they don't break, we hit them with rocks." His blue eyes gleamed. "It's fun!"

"But, honey, you'll get glass all over the road. People could cut their feet! You don't just break bottles!"

Amal looked quizzically at me. She could not understand my English, but she recognized my tone of voice. "Leave him, Audra. They are playing. They are boys!"

I rolled my eyes. "Where is Madison?" I asked Jack.

"She's with the girls. They're playing with the baby goats."

"Tell Madison we will leave soon." I squeezed Jack's arm firmly. "No more bottle-breaking," I warned softly.

Jack looked disappointed as he handed me the empty water cup. "All right," he sighed. Then he scampered back to the boys waiting by the doorway. They went out to the alley together.

"You must come to visit me every day until you leave. Every day, please, Audra!" Amal grasped my arm tightly. "You will come tomorrow?"

"I will come as much as I can, Amal." I felt the pinch of her clutching hand. My visits seemed to whet her appetite for more. I leaned back against the wall and sipped my small glass of hot tea. I felt blessed to share these women's lives but inadequate to meet their needs. My thoughts went back to the beach in Hudaydah and our futile efforts to save Herbert. I felt small, like a bucket of water when an ocean was needed.

A few days later the midmorning sun burned through my dark balto as Jaden and I walked home from our errand to town. "I'm hungry." Jaden stopped in front of a small baqala [grocery]. Can we get a snack?"

I looked at my watch. "I guess so. But we need to make it quick. These vegetables are getting heavy, and my feet hurt. We need to get home before the sun gets too hot."

"Yeah, and you have to tell me what happens to Squiggles." I nodded, glad for the break so I could contemplate the next lines of my latest story. I often created story adventures to keep the children entertained on our walks into town.

Jaden put his coconut cookies and mango juice on the shop counter. I added a bottle of water and handed the shopkeeper two hundred riyalls. The shopkeeper handed me back twenty as change. I looked at him.

"*Baqee arba'een* [There remains forty more]," I said.

The shopkeeper held my eye for a second, looked at my purchase and then back at me. "*Eshreen bas* [twenty only]."

I clenched my teeth and added each item out loud. "This makes one hundred forty riyalls. I gave you two hundred. You owed me sixty, but you gave me only twenty. I want the rest of my money. Baqee arba'een." I drilled the counter with my fingers.

The shopkeeper hesitated a second longer, then opened his cash drawer. "Tiyeb [Okay]," he grunted, handing me forty riyalls.

"*Hadtha aib* [This is shameful]," I declared. He shrugged his shoulders and turned his back to me.

I handed Jaden the bag of cookies and juice, angrily breaking the seal on my water bottle as we walked outside. "I can't believe he tried to do that," I muttered.

"Can you finish telling me about Squiggles?" Jaden asked, munching a cookie.

"In a minute. I need to remember where we are." I walked down the street, taking Jaden's hand, still fuming over the shopkeeper's change. I had seen shopkeepers count change for other women, women who could not read or write, add or subtract. Those women relied on the honesty of the men. They were treated as ignorant because they were kept ignorant.

"Well, I know better!" I said out loud.

Jaden looked puzzled. "Know what, Mommy? I think you were at the part where Squiggles was trying to get acorns up the big oak tree."

I looked blankly at him. "Oh, yes. Let's see. Squiggles had found a treasure chest of acorns but he wasn't sure how to handle them alone." I continued the story as Jaden and I walked on our way.

A motorcycle roared up the street, passing close beside us as we walked. Its rider, a young man in his twenties, wore a dirty T-shirt and a ragged futa. His turbaned *mushedda* [prayer shawl] flapped around his head. He roared past, then turned completely around in his seat. A grin leered from his yellow teeth as his eyes traveled up and down my balto. His motorcycle lunged sideways before he jerked it forward to recover himself.

"Wow, he almost fell off his motorcycle!" Jaden exclaimed.

"Yeah, well, he should have fallen off!" I spat the words out angrily and glared at the motorcycle as it faded in the distance. I was noticeably pregnant, fully covered in my balto and hejab, and I was walking with my eight-year-old son. The man ogled me as if I were wearing a bikini in a red-light district.

I jerked Jaden's hand and marched on. I had seen men ogle other women on the streets, women who were veiled and fully covered, who modestly followed the confines of their religion. But I had never expected to be treated like them.

"So how did Squiggles get help with all those acorns?" Jaden asked impatiently, struggling to keep pace with me.

"What? Oh, yes." I sighed and slowed down my walk. "I need to finish the story, don't I, honey?"

That afternoon I sat in my rocking chair watching the sun sprinkle shadows through the leaves outside my window. I was still stinging from the motorcyclist's leer and the shopkeeper's dishonesty.

"I can't believe these women put up with this, Lord!" I grumbled at the ceiling.

I drummed the arm of my chair and thought about the women I had met. I saw Amal, weary yet anxious to produce more Muslim sons to achieve her entrance into paradise. I flinched at her hunger for love, which she tried to get from me. Demanding that I visit at least twice every week, she became hurt when I could not.

I thought about Hadil's pleading eyes. She begged me to return for her wedding and witness her day of honor. I wondered if there would be other days of honor for her.

I remembered Nasimah's eyes and wondered what her dreams had been and how she had lost them. Had she dreamed of freedom from her father's control only to find more under her husband's? Had she dreamed her husband would love her?

I thought of Nabila and her malnourished son in their lean-to hut. I wondered how many other children she would have who would die.

I thought of all the other illiterate women, women kept in ignorance and treated as nothing else.

Tears filled my eyes. *How can they stand it, Lord? How can they live being treated that way?*

I let the tears trickle down my cheeks. The shadows on the floor blurred together. Then light poured through me like a bolt. *They did not know.* The women lived that way because they did not know anything else. They did not know they were valued and loved by God, that He had created them intentionally with a beautiful plan for their lives. They did not know they were worth more than gold to God—that they were worth the life of His own Son.

How could they know? No one had ever told them.

I sobbed into my hands. *Lord, send help! We cannot tell them by ourselves. We are no match for their need.* I thought about the mission group that had cancelled. *Lord, can't they reschedule? Can't You send them again? We are only a few buckets of water when the people need an ocean. Help them come, Lord. Help them come.*

14

I leaned back against my airplane headrest and closed my eyes. Madison and Jack were seated on either side of me. Jaden was next to Jack. Our next stop would be Dallas, and then a short flight from there would take us home. I swallowed the lump in my throat. Kevin would join us after five and a half weeks.

He had held me as I cried at the airport. "I don't want anything to happen to you, Audra." His voice had choked. "Time will pass quickly. You'll see. I'll be there before you know it."

I settled in for the long flight and patted my enormous abdomen. "You had better wait for your daddy," I whispered.

The children and I stayed as busy as we could during the next several weeks. We enjoyed two snowstorms. The children had forgotten snow, so I taught them how to make snow angels. They did not need to be taught how to make snowballs. We drank hot chocolate and baked cookies from pre-made dough. I was amazed by ready-to-cook food, since I cooked everything from scratch in Yemen.

I took the children to the local discount store. Giggly with excitement, they hurried down the toy aisles, but their eager eyes were soon anxious and overwhelmed. They walked wordlessly, clutching their money from their grandparents.

"Mommy, can we go home?" Madison asked. The other two nodded.

"Don't you want to buy something?" I asked, surprised.

They shook their heads. "We want to go home."

I understood. I had felt the same way when I had to choose cereal in the cereal aisle at the grocery store. "We'll shop another day," I said.

The church-provided guesthouse was warm and comfortable. But changing from the heat of Hudaydah to a west-Texas winter brought prompt sore throats and chest colds. The children and I spent consecutive Mondays in a doctor's office. Then it was my turn. A week before Kevin was due home, I became ill with fever, shivering under blankets as friends helped care for the children. I was diagnosed with a severe viral respiratory infection.

Kevin's return was a grand celebration. The children sat in Kevin's lap and showed him pictures they had colored and photographs I had taken of the snow.

"Is our house okay? Did you go to our beach? Are my shells still in the yard?" The children drilled Kevin about Yemen.

Kevin assured them that everything was fine in Yemen. I listened from my recliner. Coughing but no longer feverish, I smiled, grateful that Kevin had arrived before our baby, who would be delivered in five days via C-section.

On the morning of the scheduled delivery, the nurse buckled the fetal monitor around my bulging abdomen. "It's a good thing you're scheduled for a C-section this morning. You're in labor."

I shifted uncomfortably on the gurney. "I thought so. I guess she's waited as long as she can wait."

"She?" The nurse glanced at the screen overhead. "That heartbeat sounds like a boy."

"No! She has to be a girl!" I said. "I smocked pretty little dresses and bonnets for her!"

The nurse laughed. "Whatever you say." She was still chuckling when she wheeled me into the operating room.

An hour later we heard the first cries of our infant son. "That is the best sound in the world!" My words choked on my tears as I squeezed Kevin's hand.

The nurse held our son closer for me, and I reached out to touch his chubby fists. He wailed in his hastily wrapped blanket. I tried to soothe him. "Mommy's here, sweetheart."

"Good gracious, his voice sounds husky," I told the nurse. I wanted to take him in my arms. "It's okay, darling. Mommy's here."

The pediatrician took him to his exam table. I called to him and the nurse. "Is he okay? Is he healthy?"

"Good Apgar," the pediatrician answered. "Everything looks fine so far." He finished aspirating him and handed him to the nurses, who took him to be cleaned and weighed.

A short time later I was wheeled to recovery. Kevin stood beside me, calling the children on his cell phone, and then calling family and friends. Tears of joy poured down my cheeks. The nurses chuckled as they put a second box of tissues by my side. They seemed as joyful as I was.

I could not wait to hold my son. I had worried about the complications I had suffered and my added risk of age. But now I was immersed in gratitude. Our baby appeared healthy and normal, and I praised God

"Well, now you can say, 'my three sons.'" I grinned at Kevin.

His eyes danced. "My three sons and my beautiful wife and daughter. God is good."

Two hours later I was still waiting to hold my son. I buzzed the nurses' station. "Will they bring my baby soon? The nurse said it would be about an hour, and it's been almost two."

"I know, Mrs. Shelby. His body temperature has been a little slow to get up where it needs to be. They'll bring him in as soon as he's warmed up enough."

I thanked her reluctantly. I was eager to hold my baby and count his tiny fingers and toes. I wanted to see whose nose he had and if he had curls like his brothers. I wanted him in my arms, where he belonged.

At the end of my third hour of waiting, the pediatrician called. "Mrs. Shelby, your baby is having some difficulty breathing. I want to put him on oxygen for a little while. We'll bring him to you when he's breathing better."

I fought back tears. "How long will that be? I haven't held him yet."

"I know, Mrs. Shelby. It should not be more than a couple of hours. We'll get him to you as soon as we can."

I hung up the phone, trying to keep my tears hidden from Madison, Jaden and Jack, who were watching me. Sondra, Kevin's sister, had brought them to the hospital to see me and to meet their new baby brother.

They stood nervously beside Sondra's chair. I tried to smile. "Well, guys, it's going to be a little while before you can see your baby brother. They're giving him some oxygen to help him breathe." I motioned for them. "Hey, I haven't gotten kisses yet."

Madison and Jaden walked slowly, looking cautiously at my IV lines. Jack hung back. "They'll take this out soon," I explained.

I motioned for Kevin to hand me the plastic bag in my suitcase. "I have something for you." I gave them T-shirts labelled "Big Brother" and "Big Sister." Kevin gave them blue bubblegum cigars.

"What are we going to name him?" Madison asked.

"Well, if he had been a girl, his name would have been Abigail. We haven't chosen a boy's name. Maybe Jacob and call him Jake. Or Andrew. What do you think?"

The door opened, and our pastor walked in. "Knock-knock! Congratulations!" Luke walked over to squeeze my hand before smacking Kevin on the back. "Another boy! I looked in the nursery but did not see him. I thought he might be in here with you guys."

"He was having trouble breathing, so they put him on oxygen," I explained quietly. "He's probably in the treatment area."

"Eight pounds, nine ounces. That's a good size baby!" Luke smiled. "Congratulations!"

"Thank you, Pastor. He'll be nice and cuddly like his big brothers."

My eyes glanced at the clock. It had been four hours since my baby had been born. "I just want to hold him," I whispered. "I haven't gotten to hold him yet."

Luke looked apologetic and patted my foot at the end of the bed. "I'm sorry. I know that's hard. Let me pray with you, and then I'll let you get back to visiting with your family." He prayed, then I wiped my tears and blew my nose as Luke left the room with Kevin.

"I'm hungry," Jack whispered loudly. "Can we get something to eat?"

"There's a McDonald's not too far from here," I said. "Maybe Daddy and Aunt Sondra can take you there. You can come back later to see your baby brother."

"Okay." The children seemed relieved to go.

I dozed in and out, watching the white-faced clock on the wall. Kevin came back with Sondra and the children. Madison and Jaden grinned proudly as they presented a ceramic truck filled with blue and white carnations. A tiny white bear peeked out from the center. "This is for you, Mommy." Madison smiled.

"It's beautiful! Thank you, guys!" I read the attached card and let my eyes drift back to the clock. Seven hours had passed since my baby had been born. I had still not been able to hold him. I called the nurses' station.

"Have you heard anything about my baby?" I asked. "Do you know how much longer it's going to be?"

"I don't know, Mrs. Shelby. I'll call the nursery again. I'm sure they'll bring him to you as soon as they can."

Minutes later the phone rang. It was the pediatrician, Dr. Carey. "Mrs. Shelby, your baby has viral pneumonia. He is struggling to breathe and needs to be on a respirator. I want to transfer him to the NICU at the medical center in the city. They specialize in respiratory illnesses in newborns. They pioneered the use of the jet ventilator."

I burst into tears and motioned for Sondra to take the children outside. "Is he going to be okay?" I whispered to the pediatrician. Kevin took my hand and held it.

"The sooner we can get him to the city, the better chance he will have. It looks like he might be going into septic shock. I've called the transfer team. They should be here in about an hour. You'll have to sign some paperwork." He paused. "Mrs. Shelby, are you okay?"

I choked on my tears and answered with difficulty. "Yes."

"I'm so sorry, Mrs. Shelby. My wife and I will be praying for him and for you. Please let me know if I can do anything else for your family."

"Okay." I struggled for words. "Thank you."

I hung up the phone and wept uncontrollably. Stumbling through tears, I tried to explain to Kevin what the pediatrician had said. Kevin sat on the edge of my bed, his face pale as he held my hand and offered me tissues.

Two hours later the emergency transfer nurse wheeled our newborn son into our room. He had been placed on a portable ventilator and was lying on his side, sleeping. I looked at my little son through the thick plastic glass of his travel incubator. I reached out to touch it, longing to cradle him in my arms.

"Mrs. Shelby?" The nurse pulled a pen from her green scrub shirt. "We need you to sign these papers allowing us to transfer him." Her voice softened. "He's resting now that he's on the vent. The little guy was having a hard time trying to breathe." She touched my arm with the pen. "Ma'am, we need to get him transferred as soon as possible. The quicker we can get him settled, the better chance he'll have."

I pulled my hand slowly from the incubator. I did not bother to wipe the tears that were streaming down my cheeks. I signed the papers, one after the other, and handed the clipboard to the nurse. I wiped my face on my hospital gown.

"Madison and Jaden? Jack?" I cleared my throat and motioned as they stood with Sondra in the corner of the room. "You want to see your baby brother?"

I raised my eyes to the nurse, who nodded. "Yeah, guys," the nurse said. "Come see your brother. You gotta come quickly though. Oh," she looked at me. "We need the baby's name."

I looked at Kevin. "Jacob or Andrew. It's your call."

"Jacob. We'll call him Jake," Kevin answered.

"Jacob Shelby it is," the nurse said. "Okay, guys. Blow kisses. We're going to take him to the city and get him all better. Dad, do you want to follow us in your car?" Without waiting for an answer, the NICU nurse rolled our newborn son out of my room and toward the ambulance that waited on the dark street below.

Kevin followed them to the city hospital twenty miles away. He returned to my room about ten o'clock that night. "They got him settled, and the neonatologist examined him. He said he's a pretty sick little guy. He warned me that he will get worse before he gets better. He has viral pneumonia and is in septic shock."

He took a deep breath. "They've put him on a jet ventilator and they're monitoring him around the clock. The doc said that newborns can get sicker and sicker and then all of a sudden turn around and start getting well. Jake just needs to make it to that turnaround place."

Tears streamed down my face as I nodded. "I just want to hold him, Kevin. My arms hurt. They literally ache to hold him."

Kevin put his arms around me. "I know, honey," he whispered. I wept against his chest.

Even with the sedative the doctor had ordered, I slept very little. I jumped every time a nurse entered the room to take my temperature. I was glad when the night had ended and Kevin walked into my room the next morning.

"Good morning, sweetheart. Clear liquids, yum!" Kevin looked over my breakfast tray.

I pushed the tray aside. "How is he?" I asked.

"Well, like the neonatologist predicted, he got worse during the night." Kevin hesitated and pulled three instant snapshots from his shirt pocket. "The NICU nurses sent these for you."

I took the photographs from his hand, poring over Jake's tiny body in each one. "What's on his eyes and ears?" I asked.

Kevin cleared his throat. "Jake has begun to revert into Persistent Fetal Circulation, the blood patterns of the womb, which means there's not enough blood going to his lungs to give him the oxygen he needs." He took my hand.

"They are trying to force him out of that by simulating the womb, so they put those mufflers over his ears and the blinder across his eyes. It's dangerous, honey. Once babies go into that, they rarely come out."

I nodded, cradling the snapshots. Kevin continued. "Pastor Luke came out last night, and we prayed together over him. Jake's NICU nurse joined us. She came right up and took our hands while we were praying. She's a Christian." He smiled.

Tears glistened in my eyes. "God is good," I whispered. "He raises up His people where we need them."

"Can I get you some more ice?" Kevin asked. "Do you need anything?"

"I need to hold my baby," I whispered, clutching the snapshots to my chest.

"I know. I was looking at Jake this morning in his incubator. I wanted to reach in and pat his tummy. All I could think was that Jesus is holding him right now, cradling him close while we can't." Kevin's voice broke. I nodded, handing him a tissue while I took another for myself.

I was drying my hair when Kevin returned with the children. I had showered and dressed in a gown from home. My IV lines had been removed, so the children cuddled with me on the bed. They were animated, chattering about friends who had brought food and presents. I responded without listening. My thoughts were at the hospital twenty miles away.

"Don't be sad, Mommy." Jaden scowled. "We're here!"

"And I'm glad you are!" I kissed him and pulled them all close. "I'm so happy that you're with me!" But my heart was with the one who was missing.

After three stories from books and one about Squiggles, Kevin stood from his chair. "Come on, kids. Time for lunch." He waved by the door. "We'll come back and see

Mommy this afternoon. Give her a kiss good-bye!" And then to me, "We'll be back around three."

I walked the yellow halls of the maternity ward and stopped at the wide window of the nursery. The nurses were preparing to roll the babies into their mothers' rooms. One looked up as I watched through the window. She had been Jake's nurse in the O.R. She smiled slightly and waved uncertainly. I put my hand against the glass and tried to smile back. I turned and walked away. I passed doors streaming with pink or blue ribbons. My own door was bare.

Words echoed in my mind. *In remembrance of Me, heal the sick.* I frowned. The altar at church was engraved *In Remembrance of Me*, but there was no "heal the sick." I brushed the words away. I walked back into my room and sat on the edge of my bed. My arms ached, hungry for my son. Again the words echoed. *In remembrance of Me, heal the sick.*

Puzzled, I glanced at the Bible on my nightstand. I remembered Jesus' words, *"Do this in remembrance of Me."* I crossed my arms tightly around my chest. *My arms hurt, Lord.* Tears trickled down my face. *I ache to hold my baby.*

The words whispered through like a quiet song. *In remembrance of Me, heal the sick.* I knew God was speaking to me.

In remembrance of Me, heal the sick? My baby is critically ill! What do You mean, Lord? This doesn't make sense.

I rocked back and forth on my bed. My arms yearned for my child, aching to nuzzle him and whisper in his ear all I had planned. But I could not. He was twenty miles away, in another hospital, in another town.

I picked up the snapshots Kevin had brought from the NICU nurse. I looked at my newborn son, covered by a profusion of IV lines and a jet ventilator tube. To force him out of the Persistent Fetal Circulation, he had been chemically paralyzed. Yellow mufflers covered his ears, and a blue blinder hid his eyes. He was under orders for minimal stimulation; no one was to touch him unnecessarily.

I tossed the snapshots on the bed. "Lord, even if I was there, I could not hold him," I wailed. "Even if I was right there beside him, I could not cuddle him close to my heart. There's a barrier between us!"

At that moment it was as if the fingers of God snapped in my ears. He whispered, "Yes, Audra. There are millions of babies, adult babies, teenage babies I long to hold close to My heart and tell them all that I have planned for them. But there is a barrier between us. They are separated from Me by a disease called sin."

I sat stock-still. The words I had heard made sense. *In remembrance of Me, heal the sick.* I sat in quiet awe, pondering what I had just been shown. It was a sacred and intimate moment, a glimpse into the heart of God.

Tears streamed onto my gown as I looked toward the ceiling. "Help me never to forget, Lord," I wept. "Help me to remember this pain. It's Your pain, Lord. Use me to heal the sick. Help me to live in remembrance of You."

That afternoon one of my prayer partners came to visit. Kathy presented me with a huge mass of blue ribbons adorned with a small white teddy bear and a banner emblazoned, "It's a boy!" She hung it firmly on the door and handed me a gift bag. "Congratulations on the birth of your son!"

I was startled and stumbled for words. Everyone had been afraid to mention Jake. "Thank you," I whispered. Kathy gave me a hug and left as quickly as she had come.

I followed her to the door. I touched the blue ribbons streaming in shiny profusion. I looked around at the pride displayed on other doors, and I straightened my shoulders.

"I had a baby, too," I whispered. "I have a son!" In the pain of the circumstances, I had forgotten the blessing.

I had given birth to an eight-pound, nine-ounce baby boy. I had a reason to celebrate. "Thank you, Kathy," I whispered.

I stopped at the nurses' station. "I need to get a breast pump," I told the nurse. "I need to store milk for my son."

The nurse looked at me uneasily. All of the nurses had been hesitant, uncertain how to act. They knew how ill my baby was and understood his limited chance of survival.

"Okay, Mrs. Shelby," she said finally. "We'll get you one right a way."

I left the hospital the next day. It was earlier than my obstetrician preferred, but he relented, knowing I wanted to see my baby. He discharged me with strong warnings about rest and recovery. I went straight to the hospital in Odessa.

Jacob was crying in his NICU incubator when I approached him. He was on his jet ventilator, but his blinders and ear mufflers had been removed. His tiny face was puckered as tears streamed down from his squinting eyes, but no sound came from his mouth. The jet ventilator prevented it. I could see him crying, but I could not hear him.

Tears streamed down my face as I gripped the side of the incubator. "When you are free, little Jake, and I can hold you in my arms, I will never let you cry again without being there to hold you through it. Never," I promised.

For the next several days I was pulled between my children at home and my infant son in the city. When Jacob was nine days old, he was taken off the ventilators and placed in my arms for the first time. I took him carefully, trying not to disturb the IV lines that still remained.

"Hi, sweetheart," I whispered. "I'm your mommy!"

Hearing my voice, Jake stretched his tiny face toward mine. He broke into a wide, ear-to-ear grin. "He knows his mommy!" I sobbed. "He knows it's me!"

The nurse bustled around Jake's crib. "Oh, all newborns smile periodically. It's just gas." But I knew better. My son knew my voice, and nothing would convince me otherwise. His wide smile was my reward for waiting endlessly to hold him.

Two months later we prepared our family of six to return to Yemen. I packed baby clothes into foot lockers, stopping periodically to bend over Jake's portable cradle. He was sleeping on his side, his gentle breath soft and even. He shuddered slightly when I touched his chest.

I sank into the rocking chair to watch him. "Thank You for him, Lord," I whispered. "He is so precious to me. Help me never to forget what it felt like not to hold him."

I thought back to the hospital, to that intimate moment with God. I cherished it and held it deep within me. But it had come at a great cost.

I looked up at the ceiling. "He was my son, Lord!" My voice broke, remembering the pain I had suffered.

God quietly answered, "He was My Son, too."

It took some time for me to realize that He was not talking about Jacob.

Soon afterward, we were on the final leg of our journey back to Yemen. We leaned back in our seats as the wide-bodied plane jetted into the evening sky of Frankfurt. The trees disappeared into the German darkness far below. Jacob slept undisturbed in my arms. I held him close.

"Would you like to move to a different seat? There might be an extra one available to lay him down." The flight attendant handed me a dinner menu.

"That's okay." I smiled. "I like holding him."

Kevin winked at me from the menu he was reading to Jack. "You're going to be saying that when he's eighteen," he chuckled.

"Probably." I grinned and cuddled Jake closer.

Jake's first two months had passed quickly. He had grown chubby, much heartier than the seven-pound baby who had left the hospital after thirteen days. He had become a lusty eater with an equally lusty squall when he disliked something. I kissed his soft, pink cheek.

Madison stroked the top of his fair head. "He's so cute, Mommy," she whispered.

I nodded. "God has really blessed us, hasn't He?"

Madison leaned against my arm. "Do you think he'll be okay in Yemen?" Her ten-year-old eyes looked worried.

I moved Jake to one arm and wrapped my other one around Madison. "He'll be fine in Yemen. Haven't we been okay there? Even when you were sick, God provided what we needed, didn't He? He's enough for what we need."

I looked into her eyes. "Honey, God never tells us to go out and let Him know how things go. He tells us to go out and He will go with us. Every step of the way."

Madison smiled and leaned against me. "I'm glad we're going home to Hudaydah," she said.

"Me, too." I kissed her cheek. "Me, too."

I settled back against my seat thinking about my neighbors in Hudaydah and my friend Amal. I thought about them and the children they had lost. I watched my son breathing evenly in my arms and tried not to remember the looks from friends who questioned our return to Yemen.

Our well-meaning friends cautioned against it. Doctors warned that Jake could have pneumonia at least eight times during his first two years, reminding us that he was vulnerable to Sudden Infant Death syndrome.

"Jacob's life does not belong to us," I had responded. "God intervened and spared his life. They call him the miracle baby, remember? His life belongs to God."

I closed my eyes, reliving the pain of my empty arms. I heard again the words, *In remembrance of Me, heal the sick.*

"Lord, help me never to forget the *why* of what we do. Help me to remember that pain of separation and to see people as You see them, to know Your desire to hold each one close."

I thought about the news we had received from the International Mission Board. A young college graduate had arrived in Yemen to join our work in the Tihama. Scott was waiting for us in Hudaydah, where he had committed to serve for two years.

Jake stirred softly in his sleep. A smile briefly touched his lips. I kissed his fuzzy head. I did not know what the future would hold for him or our family, but I was confident in not knowing. I knew who held us in His hands, and I had found Him faithful to walk us through any situation we could possibly face.

I chuckled, thinking of the women who were waiting in Hudaydah. They would be pleased that I was returning with a son. Amal would cradle Jake and pass him for other women to kiss and pinch as we sipped hot tea and munched popcorn. I shivered with excitement. *Lord, I'll tell them Jacob's story. I'll tell them how deeply You love them.*

I leaned against my headrest, thinking back to our arrival in Yemen three years before. I remembered my first yearning to know the women, to get behind the veils of Yemen. "Lord," I whispered. "Your people prayed, and You opened the door into the lives of these women. Take me behind their veils again. I'm ready to show them Your heart."

Watching the bored eyes of fellow college students during an evangelism training course, Audra swallowed back tears. "Lord, these are the most powerful words on earth, but they have become clichés. Use me to communicate them in a way that people will understand." Little did Audra Grace Shelby* know where that request would lead.

Audra began her missionary experience as a three-month-old, when her parents were commissioned as missionaries to South America. When Audra was five, her mother died tragically in childbirth at the end of the family's first term. Her widowed father returned to the United States with his five children, ages seven years and under. Five years later the family returned to the mission field with a new stepmother and a new place of service: the Caribbean.

Audra met her husband, Kevin*, in Texas, where she worked as a children's editor for religious curricula, writing and editing Bible stories and studies for children and teachers. After her daughter, Madison*, and sons, Jaden* and Jack*, were born, Audra began a desktop publishing business out of her home and continued writing and editing, while developing her interests in heirloom sewing and design, and gardening.

Kevin and Audra and their three young children left their home in Texas to answer God's call to Yemen. They were appointed as missionaries with the International Mission

Board S.B.C. to Yemen, where Audra spent treasured afternoons sharing the lives of Muslim women and reaching behind their veils to communicate God's love and message in a way they could understand. Audra used her sewing skills among illiterate women and continued writing articles about the people of Yemen and creating stories for her children. The family returned briefly to the United States for the birth of their fourth child, Jacob.*

When the educational and social needs of their growing children became difficult to meet in Yemen, the family transferred to Egypt. Two years later, the family returned to the United States, where their oldest children entered high school. Audra and Kevin celebrate 24 years of marriage and remain actively involved in getting God's message into the Middle East through global ministries and outreach opportunities. Audra continues to write and speak in churches and conferences across the nation, pursuing her passion to communicate who God is in a way people understand.

Visit Audra at her website and blog, www.audragrace shelby.com, and at www.facebook.com/audragrace.shelby, where you will also find her current speaking schedule and information for scheduling conferences and speaking engagements.

* Audra's name, as well as the names of her family, have been changed to protect friends and ongoing work in the Middle East.